972
Ari
Ari

D0778763

COLUMBIA BIBLE COLLEC

444 00037 6137

ARISTIDE
AN AUTOBIOGRAPHY

ARISTIDE
AN AUTOBIOGRAPHY

Jean-Bertrand Aristide
with Christophe Wargny

Translation by Linda M. Maloney

ORBIS BOOKS

Maryknoll, New York 10545

Second Printing, April 1993

The Catholic Foreign Mission Society of America (Maryknoll) recruits and trains people for overseas missionary service. Through Orbis Books, Maryknoll aims to foster the international dialogue that is essential to mission. The books published, however, reflect the opinions of their authors and are not meant to represent the official position of the society.

Originally published as *Tout homme est un homme.* Copyright © 1992 Editions du Seuil, 27, rue Jacob, Paris F-75261

English translation copyright © 1993 by Orbis Books

All rights reserved

Published by Orbis Books, Maryknoll, NY 10545

Manufactured in the United States of America

Library of Congress Cataloging-in-Publication Data

Aristide, Jean-Bertrand.
    [Tout homme est un homme. English]
    Aristide : an autobiography / Jean-Bertrand Aristide with
Christophe Wargny ; translation by Linda M. Maloney.
      p. cm.
    ISBN 0-88344-845-9
    1. Aristide, Jean-Bertrand. 2. Haiti—Politics and
government—1986 3. Presidents—Haiti—Biography. 4. Catholic
Church—Haiti—Clergy—Biography. I. Wargny, Christophe.
II. Title.
F1928.23.A75A3   1993
972.9407'3'092—dc20
[B]   92-34558
                                        CIP

Go toward other mornings of love, other mid-summer days, toward a life newly begun. Now you know, as I do, what lies within the belly of misery, . . . why, every day, there are new tears in their eyes, why the people do not know how to read, why men leave their native lands, why maladies are ravaging our people, why little girls become prostitutes. . . .

Jacques Stephen Alexis
Compère général soleil

Contents

I

Introduction

CHAPTER 1

The Second Independence

Mwen leve menm devan Bondye ak devan Nasyon an, map mache dapre konstitisyon an, dapre tout lwa peyi a. Map fè tout moun suiv yo. Map respekte tout dwa pèp ayisyen an. Map chèche fè tout moun respekte yo tou . . .

With a quiet gesture the new president, a little frail, raises his right hand: "I swear before God and before the nation that I will respect the constitution and the laws of the country and will make everyone follow them. I will respect the rights of the Haitian people and take care to have them respected by everyone. . . ."

Ertha Pascal Trouillot, a mulatto aristocrat dressed all in white, who, for almost a year, had served as interim president, had just completed her task. Jean-Bertrand Aristide, elected on December 16, 1990, succeeded to the presidency on February 7, 1991. The National Assembly, also newly chosen by the voters, gathered in a body in its assembly hall to hear the presidential address. The atmosphere, which was serious and a little strained, led onlookers to forget the celebration that was beginning outside. An enthusiasm and festive rejoicing had inundated the country for many days. The people were counting on a change.

The annual carnival, which usually unfolded just before Mardi Gras, began several days earlier that year. Groups of townspeople, especially young ones, were bustling every-

where. For those who arrived in Port-au-Prince, the scene
between the airport and the populous parts of the inner city,
viewed through the open windows of a rattletrap taxi, presented the same depressing picture as ever: this city is a
sewer. The swerving of the vehicle, protecting its future and
that of its proprietor by avoiding the gigantic and yawning
potholes, confirms the diagnosis. The worn streets traverse
or skirt huge slums completely exposed to the ravages of tropical rainstorms, but at the same time suffering from a scarcity
of water, suffocating heat, and pestilential odors arising from
overcrowding. Hygiene? Unknown. The piles of refuse accumulate and waste water flows between the tin houses of the
slums, rusty or shining in the sun.

In forty years the population of Port-au-Prince has increased tenfold, and the city now has more than one and a
half million inhabitants. But the excessive centralization has
not been accompanied by any advance preparation for receiving more than a hundred thousand new townspeople every
year into these inhuman conditions. Want of foresight, contempt, madness, chaos, anarchy—the lack of any urban policy
or public hygiene has lent this agglomeration a look of des-
olation and of contrast.

This is how Jean Metellus, a contemporary Haitian writer,
sees it:

> Alongside the houses of the bourgeoisie, architectural
> beauties whose inhabitants bathe in freshness and ease
> from morning to evening, hidden within colorful and
> verdant gardens with a variety of fruit trees ... [are]
> miserable dwellings built of scavenged materials, utterly
> unhealthful, without utilities, lighted with kerosene, at
> the mercy of the first strong wind, vulnerable to fire,
> without sanitation and without water, burned by the sun
> from morning to evening.[1]

This time committees, formed four months ago to support
Father Aristide's candidacy, have undertaken a sweeping

clean-up campaign, a huge laundering operation that reflects (to borrow from the richly metaphorical Creole language) a general clean sweep, the purifying torrent, *lavalas* in Creole, promised by the supporters of the newly elected president. Armed with shovels, rakes, brooms or brushes, they pack the streets, livening up the telephone poles, the walls, the facades with blue and red paint: even the sidewalks, where there are any.

An artistic people, excelling in naive painting, the Haitians produce frescoes of human dimensions, using whatever materials come to hand. Titid, as he is called by his supporters, appears here and there, with his short hair and thin mustache, with or without his glasses, on the walls of the city. He is in turn serene, detached, smiling, pensive or radiant.

The capital city is absorbed in fixing itself up. Everyone is invited to donate a few *gourdes* — the Haitian currency — for dressing the most visible wounds or adding color to the gloom of an environment to which no one has paid any attention for a long time. Haiti is now receiving visitors — a rare moment. While the Western democracies or the neighboring countries have shown timidity or complacency in the face of successive dictatorships, leaders of these countries have never travelled here. There has never been a question of placing one's finger — or one's foot — on one of the warts of the American continent.

The invited guests have come: Carlos Andrés Pérez, the president of Venezuela, former president Jimmy Carter from the United States, and Madame Danièle Mitterrand, the moving spirit of France-Libertés, representing her husband who had to remain in Paris "on account of the international situation." But they are not exactly a crowd. Looking closely at the list, one could, with the exception of the Caribbean nations, almost speak of indifference, if not of a boycott.

The international situation is especially tense and is drawing all eyes toward Baghdad and Kuwait City. The war in the Gulf has just begun. But is that a sufficient explanation? At the hour of the bankruptcy of communism and the triumph of the West and its democratic model, "in charge and sure of himself," is President Aristide, the one they have been waiting for, in Washington or in Paris, to put an end to the crisis in Haiti?

Six years have passed since Duvalier's dictatorship dissolved amid popular rejoicing. Since then, elections have been manipulated or prevented by coups d'état, and the West has been searching in vain for a person or a system that might be acceptable. The generals have scarcely been helpful in solving this difficult equation, recklessly wielding the stick, breaking even the most insignificant promises—and aggravating still more the plight of the most impoverished people in the Americas. Located between Martinique and Puerto Rico, Haitians have a standard of living close to that of the countries of the African Sahel!

Out of this bleakness arose a man who refused to compromise, who demanded a merciless struggle against the consequences of dictatorship and all it left in its wake, especially the all-too-famous Tontons Macoute, the military arm of Duvalierism. In short, a man who wants to create a clean slate: a man who is more than merely a man. In a profoundly Catholic country, a priest, and one whom the Haitians consider a prophet.

We won!—and that collective "we" is not demagoguery: the triumphant election of the priest was above all an act by which Haitians exorcised their own special demons.[2] In a country that often gives the impression of combining all the disadvantages of Africa with those of the Americas and in a vicious circle of underdevelopment and unbridled individualism, this extraordinary and magical relationship may have been either the cause of many false steps or the source of new experiences.

Can liberation theology, which has now attained the summit of power through the election to national office of one of its "delegates" deal with the consequences? Accustomed to combatting corrupt systems, can liberation theology propose an alternative kind of government?

Aristide might have wished to assume total power. Wasn't he elected in a sufficiently overwhelming manner for that to happen? Yet nothing in his style or in his electoral campaign indicated any desire on his part to become a dictator. He said that his voters should not hesitate to call him to account. Haiti's desire today is to evolve toward a democratic system.

Aristide was reluctant to put himself forward. It was the unbearable void created by the cowardice of the parties that led to his decision. The country may be deceived, and the president may yield to the temptation to become a dictator. The fact remains that he did not present himself as having that intention, and he was not elected for that purpose. This is an absolutely new proposition in the history of this country!

So wrote Gérard Barthélemy, a French ethnologist living in Haiti for the past ten years.[3]

Aristide's origins also distinguish him from the politicians: he is not a member of the dominant class. His abiding and exclusive concern for the marginal, what liberation theologians call the preferential option for the poor, has changed him into a spokesperson for the damned of the earth—the eighty percent in Haiti who live below the threshold of absolute poverty. He also differs from his confrères in the church or in politics because he is confronted daily with the reality he denounces. He speaks the language of the people, fired by an exceptional charisma. Like Saint-Just, he believes what he says. And he says everything that he believes. He says it in Creole, a language of humor and of many images. This man, imbued with a faith and a force of conviction that are extraordinary—who is able alternately to reassure and to disturb—occupies a place that, anywhere else, would be contested by politicians or media professionals. He has slowly built up a power without any structure, alongside a great many structures that are utterly lacking in power.

Is he a demagogue, a visionary, a communist, a mixture of

Robin Hood, Robespierre and Che Guevara, as his opponents say? Perhaps he is, at least as far as courage is concerned, even if he draws on it today more than the examples cited above. Neither repression nor death worries him; instead, they reinforce and stimulate him. Truly a miraculous survivor after nine failed assassination attempts, he seems more than ever to be the last pure soul in the country.

Apart from being a highly gifted student, nothing predestined him to govern his country. The last hope of a people crushed by thirty-five years of terror, illiteracy and underdevelopment, at the same time beloved to the point of idolatry, he was caught, in 1990, in the meshes of his own commitment. Withdrawal, something he often dreamed about, became impossible. He had done too much, said too much. He understood all too well the residents of the slums, he felt all too well the claims of those without work and without shelter. He had spoken too much in the name of those who could never speak. To refuse, to abdicate, would have been a betrayal.

Even though he has a feeling for words and for a crowd, combined with unlimited stubbornness, Aristide does not possess the physique of a John Paul II, a Fidel Castro or a Lech Walesa. He sometimes succumbs briefly to depression. He has nothing in common with those jugglers, those heavyweights of the prize ring, the real stars of the show: he is a thin young man with the physical appearance of a student, lanky, scrawny, as if he has not finished growing. But the sparkling eyes behind the steel-rimmed glasses speak of determination, a candor mixed with caustic humor. The priest's apparent serenity quickly gives way to a style of argument that is imperturbable, implacable, and accusing.

A Don Quixote attacking those more powerful than he, Aristide ought to be dead by now. The miracle-man of St. Jean Bosco, whose church was set on fire by the Macoutes in the middle of Mass, has never spared his opponents. The idea that compromise could be possible, or even necessary, never made any headway before 1990, the year in which the collusion between the Macoutes and the army appeared to be weakening.

Two enemies who sought in vain to eliminate him physically joined with two others whom he denounced for their connivance with the established order of things: the United States government and the Catholic hierarchy, who were jointly suspected or accused of putting pressure on the people to accept their lot with resignation.

Never had defiance, even hostility, toward the hierarchy of the church (Haitian or Roman) been pressed so far, a consequence of its failure to *re-form*, to reduce the distance between the head and the body. The two are terribly out of step, and the ideas of Leonardo Boff appear to have found a fertile field in Haiti in which their subversive character could be pushed to the extreme.

Gérard Barthélémy also recalls this was used by both the candidate and the president:

> The Haitian electorate, in voting for Aristide, turned to its own profit the election that was more or less imposed on it from outside. The circumstances thus aided the emergence of a candidate chosen by the people themselves, for Aristide is not a traditional leader who imposes himself on those below, but is largely the creation, the emanation of the people. In thus acting, the people gave their own significance to the election, both as to its form and its content.

One can readily understand that in 1990 such an individual would not be the favorite or the choice of the Western governments. The denunciation of U. S. imperialism or of the Macoute lords does not conjure up the image of a political realist, someone tolerant or even socially acceptable!

The democracy thus promised would undoubtedly not be a Haitian version of the liberal or classical parliamentary systems. Much like a Walesa or a Václav Havel, but with even more risk in a country where life is so cheap, this man is a "refusenik," an insurgent, a rebel whom the Haitians had chosen and elected. Is there some significance for Western democracy in the torrent, the *lavalas*, that now must be channeled? Can the wave that broke against the Macoutes' plundering, against "a parasitical and predatory state,"[4] be compared to the wall of Stalinism crushed in Europe by popular pressure?

The Haitian people who pressed into the festive capital in tens of thousands to see and hear Titid did not care. The second stage of his investiture was a *Te Deum* sung in the cathedral in Port-au-Prince. Fifteen hundred invited persons were able to squeeze in; others in the church square had to content themselves with watching through the open door.

Before the altar, young girls sang in Creole. Behind them, in the apse, the Haitian bishops, most of them accomplices in Duvalierism, sat very quietly in their seats next to Jacques Gaillot, the bishop of Évreux and the champion of the opposition within the French episcopacy. He said, "No one can halt the destiny of a people. I think that the bishops and Rome will rejoice with me." We may, of course, have some doubts whether the French prelate's declaration was truly shared by all his colleagues!

The homily by Bishop Pétion-Laroche, president of the Haitian Episcopal Conference, was rendered inaudible by a defective microphone, but it proclaimed the reconciliation of the bishops, more opportunist than ever, with a man whom they had so often held up to public obloquy!

In the first row in the nave sat the generals, in their straps and braid, their shoulders bound with lanyards: men who had built their whole careers on Duvalier. They did not know it yet, but the priest-president had decided to make them the first victims — less pitiable than their own — of the new regime.

The third act, the best attended, took place at the national palace. The enormous edifice stands out by its almost immaculate whiteness, in the middle of the Champ de Mars, a few steps from the Dessalines barracks and the gloom of the central city. The crowd had been waiting for hours to hear Titid's speech. The people were making themselves heard at the expense of the military: *"Pèp la inosan, Abraham, rele san manman w yo, pale yo, nou pap pran nan kou deta ankò"* ("The people are innocent, Abraham; let the mercenaries know that we are not going to accept any more coups d'état").

The diplomats and invited guests were all present. No one would be disappointed or misled. The multilingual president greeted the peoples of Latin America in Spanish and, fortified by the 67 percent of the votes obtained in an election whose validity no one contested, the Haitian flea challenged the American mastodon: "Don't be afraid!"

The speech moved from French to Creole, and Titid announced to the crowd that all the generals except Hérard Abraham, whose loyalty had been manifested a month earlier, were "to be retired to remove any cause for discord between the army and the people." The floods of people who had been demonstrating in the streets of Port-au-Prince since morning were stirred up still more: *"Si nou pa kale je nou, ya volè kannon nou Seyè; si nou pa rele anmwe, ya volè kannon nou Seyè"* ("if we do not open our eyes wide, they will steal our cannon, Lord; if we do not show our discontent, they will steal our cannon, Lord").

The suddenness of the decision was surprising, but the moment was well chosen. How could the army react in the face of a man whose popularity was at its zenith and whose international legitimacy was uncontested? All the more when he shouted at them: "If the garden of security flowers, we will water it *Charlemagne Péralte*-ly in order to reap *lavalas*-ly."[5] Charlemagne Péralte was an officer who tried to resist the American occupation of Haiti before World War II.

The president explained to me a few months later: "In Creole, we say that *'pwason toujou kòmanse pouri nan tèt'* ["Fish always spoils from the head downward"]. I applied this rule first of all to the army, just as I would apply it to society. It was necessary to begin at the top." However, the medicine would be insufficient, and fundamental reforms too slow.

The essential theme of the speech was an appeal to justice and solidarity: "Does a stone in fresh water understand the suffering of a stone in the sun?" as well as to hope: may all lift their heads high! *"Tout tan tèt pa koupe, li pa dezespere mete chapo"* ("as long as the head is not cut off, it cannot give up hope of wearing a hat"). Let the children know that tomorrow they will go to school, and the poor that they will eat at least once a day, because *"Titid ak malere se marasa"* ("Titid and the poor are twins"). The theme of fraternity/sorority or marriage ("Titid and the people are married") had been the center of the electoral campaign!

The army decapitated, the Macoutes inactive since the last attack on an orphanage founded by Father Aristide, the two houses of the assembly apparently controlled by the friends of *Lavalas* (the name of the movement supporting Father Aristide): it appeared, in the winter of 1991, that the president had in his hands all the levers of control, both political and social, not counting the popular committees that were galvanizing the people's energies. This was true even if relations should change rapidly between one of the parties in parliament and the executive.

Everything was possible; everything would be possible if the country were not deprived of everything except energy and hope. This tropical country which suffers from a shortage of water (even though it rains much more than in Paris or New York), which is denuded of trees (cut down for fuel), where the earth has never produced either Havana cigars or the necessary nourishment for the bulk of the population, where unrest keeps away the tourists who are so numerous in the neighboring islands: Haiti seems to be cursed by the gods. Were two centuries of tragic and endemically violent history finally approaching an end?

The president, *Lavalas*, the movement that carried him to power, and the voters all wanted to believe it as they proclaimed together, on February 7, 1991, Haiti's second independence. Could one say, as Goethe did when witnessing the battle of Valmy, "from this day and in this place a new day is beginning; you can say, 'I was there' "?

Latin America was about to celebrate the five hundredth anniversary of its "discovery" by Christopher Columbus. There were a great many ways to celebrate or mourn that event. On February 7, 1991, Haiti, the most impoverished of all, of everything, celebrated its restored liberty, to the sound of South American music and African rhythms.

Father Aristide, at this point when the enemy appeared to be crushed or at least weakened, hoped for a nonviolent transition to democracy, accomplished more by persuasion than by force: would the presidential role allow him to transform himself from a militant advocate to an arbiter, an administrator who could guide a society through a process of perilous change? He knew, in any case, that in a delicate geopolitical context he held only two trump cards: his legitimacy and the confidence of the Haitian people. Plus there was a certain respect: in a world in which the small nations have to bow to the suzerainty of the great powers, he was not controlled or manipulated by anyone.

Jean-Bertrand Aristide, a priest cursed by the bishops, the generals and the oligarchs, is attempting in this book to explain to a people in rags that the miracles one awaits with resignation are nothing but snares and delusions, and that he can offer them nothing but justice and dignity. That is a lot: it is in itself the gateway out of hell. But in the morning, when they get out of bed, whether it is a straw mattress or the hard ground, one Haitian out of two still does not know how he or she will eat that day.

NOTES

1. Jean Metellus, *Haïti, une nation pathétique* (Paris: Denoël, 1987).
2. *Libération,* December 18, 1990.
3. Barthélemy is also the author of a remarkable work on the rural world of Haiti, *Le Pays en dehors* (Port-au-Prince: Éditions Henri Deschamps, 1989).
4. These words were used in 1990 in an internal report of the

French cooperative mission. They were quoted by *Le Monde,* July 2, 1991.

5. This is a neologism constructed from *Lavalas,* the movement that brought Aristide to power.

CHAPTER 2

The Pearl of the Antilles

The second independence is proclaimed this 7th of February 1991! But before there can be a second, there had to be a first. Almost two centuries earlier another exceptional man on the rise, Toussaint-Louverture, inspired an enslaved people to their first independence. That was in 1804! Napoleon, at the summit of his power, crowned emperor in Paris that year, could not thwart the collective emancipation of a nation of blacks.

"The rupture is the same today as at the beginning of the nineteenth century," explains Jean-Bertrand Aristide. "The political changes in 1804 resulted in a disguised colonialism. With our second independence the Haitian people must bring about a social revolution by ceasing to confuse the state with the interests of the oligarchy. For the people, utterly exploited or forgotten, the independence that now exists is only nominal."

Christopher Columbus, after visiting the Bahamas and Cuba, discovered Hispaniola in December 1492. The Indians were rapidly decimated and the island, abandoned by the Spanish in favor of the French, the English or the Dutch, passed in the seventeenth century into the hands of buccaneers and pirates. By the Treaty of Ryswick, which ended the War of the League of Augsburg in Europe in 1697, the west-

15

ern third of Saint-Domingue became a French possession. "The pearl of the Antilles," "an island worth an empire," on the eve of the French revolution accounted for one-third of France's external trade and was the essential supplier of the world's sugar! The demographic trend attests to the choice nature of the place: thirty thousand whites, an equal number of freed persons, and five hundred thousand black slaves, the majority of them recently imported.

The news of the revolution in France and the faltering of the Assemblies brought repercussions: the Jacquerie combined in a true revolution. Arriving to thwart it, the commissioners of the Convention granted freedom to all. Toussaint-Louverture built a genuine army, defeated the English, installed an administration and held a plebiscite on a constitution. The army sent by Bonaparte, though it eliminated the father of the country, was unable to halt the march of independence. On January 1, 1804, Haiti became the first black republic. The planters were massacred and the country was in ruins. It has never been rebuilt, and no wonder, since the war of independence was duplicated by the majority's rejection of the economic system then in effect.

From having been an exporting country, Haiti became a self-sustaining economy in which the peasants lived within a closed, egalitarian system. The country was quarantined by the great Western powers and forced to pay Paris a golden price for its independence. It was reduced to a vassal state, corrupt, oppressed, a permanent parasite and destabilizer. During the nineteenth century Haiti had fallen into the hands of rulers submissive to France and the United States and existed completely divorced from the industrial revolution. Under the existing system of power, the blacks generally retained political power while the tiny minority of mulattoes took charge of the economy.

The American occupation (1915–1934) fixed the country definitively within the orbit of the United States. The Monroe Doctrine was applied there as elsewhere. It was at that time that the two hundred millionaire families were established:

Haiti is today one of the countries of the world in which the hierarchy of incomes is steepest.

Economic corruption and political cynicism went hand in hand. The coup d'état of September 30, 1991, was the final manifestation of that connivance. The republic of Port-au-Prince has created fortunes and defeats governments. No one has given the least thought to the peasants—ninety percent of the population at the beginning of the century, two-thirds at the end—except to exploit them. In turn, the central power has been perceived by the rural people only as a mechanism for causing calamities.

The memory of a glorious independence and the religion of national heroes are nothing but dust thrown in the people's eyes. The successive dictatorships have made constant use of them as justifications or alibis for their deeds. The majority of Haitians perceive no road toward emancipation whatsoever.

With the advent of François Duvalier, the dictatorship took a very different form: its power became ideological and apprenticed itself to magic. The economic crisis was used as a pretext for transforming terror into a system of government. No popular movement of any kind would be tolerated in the future. The oppression became terrible, permanent, and inexorable. Duvalier made systematic use of the state's capital to pay his faithful followers and to purchase allies.

The generalized corruption allowed him to organize and pay a militia of "volunteers for national security." The Tontons Macoute broke the army's monopoly and assured the maintenance of order. The Duvaliers, father and son, presidents for life (1957–1986), constructed a unique system of oppression. The intelligentsia was decimated, the elites often forced into exile. Thirty thousand opponents were executed, many of them at Fort Dimanche, an interrogation and detention center from which no one emerged alive.

The day after his investiture, accompanied by many thousands of Haitians, President Aristide went to that old political prison, now transformed into a museum dedicated to those who disappeared under the dictatorship. A few survivors, saved by the *dechoukaj* (the uprooting and, by extension, elimination) of Jean-Claude Duvalier, were present to view, once again, the six-foot-square cells that at one time held thirty-five people each.

"In order to survive," one of them told Agence-France-Presse, "I completely forgot about everything outside for seven years and seven months — my family, my children — and concentrated totally on my life as a prisoner. Mentally, I blocked out all freedom of thought. In this way, my morale held up and my physical resistance was maintained. My father had his eyes gouged out by the fingers of a Tonton Macoute, in reprisal because they had not succeeded in arresting his son."

Max Bourjolly, the head of the United Communist Party of Haiti, adds: "We were never allowed to walk. We received one or two cups of water a day, sometimes nothing, no medical care; thousands of prisoners died of infectious diarrhea, tuberculosis, malaria and dementia related to total lack of nutrition. At night, we listened to the baying of the dogs that were digging up the corpses nearby."[1]

One part of the army and of the middle class supported Duvalier and held to their catechism. François, like so many totalitarian leaders, promoted a cult of personality and declared himself "the apostle of the common good," "the electrifier of souls," or "an immaterial being." Although a champion of *"Noirism"* (Blackness),[2] he did not eliminate the mulatto middle class which, for monetary considerations, maintained its economic position.

This vertical, terrorist, all-powerful system dreamed of breaking the old hierarchies. It did break the elite, weakened or divided the army, and placed its own men at the head of the church; it pretended to resist Uncle Sam, but played an adroit role in the struggles over Franco-American influence.

If we can believe the American Federal Reserve Bank, the Duvaliers and their clan succeeded in diverting nearly eight hundred million dollars in thirty years, which was more than a third of the total value of international assistance during that period. Jean-Claude Duvalier, in exile in France since 1986, can continue to enjoy a peaceful life there, while the Haitians await, no doubt in vain, the restitution of the stolen cash.

The abundant labor force in the slums of Port-au-Prince made possible a beginning of industrialization, in the form of assembly plants that opened at the expense of food-producing agriculture. Land speculation and the creation of one or two tourist complexes took preference over social investment (which was non-existent) or infrastructures for communication, which were in a general state of dilapidation. The French minister Robert Galley moved to Haiti to establish Coco Beach, a paradise for the rich, at the same time that the ragged poor were being invited to sell their blood to American laboratories at five dollars a liter.

Smaller than Switzerland or Belgium, Haiti shelters six to seven million inhabitants, poorer than they were ten years ago. Nearly two million Haitians live abroad. The figures always come from somewhere else, since the state itself would have great difficulty furnishing them. The pearl of the Antilles, those islands that form an arc from Mexico to Venezuela, the once-coveted horn of plenty turns its gaze, like all the others, to the American giant. Geopolitics requires it.

This is one dimension that no responsible Haitian dare forget. The Caribbean world scarcely exists. It is doubtful that Europe, once so close, is prepared to dispute this part of the world with its transatlantic ally.

This is the gloomy picture within which the Haitian people continue to live, and even to smile and dance. This kind of social landscape, as President Aristide has remarked, could have accounted for a suicide rate far above the world average, but that is not at all the case. No matter how bitter the reality, hope and struggle remain, and so does art, which plays and writes and listens.

The sad, tragic reality, transformed by vivid color, transcends itself, moving within a marvelous imaginary world which makes the human being the best remedy for the human being. We need only mention the fevered painting of those whom Jean Metellus calls "the magicians of freshness," who are "possessed by the grace of life, by justice and by compassion."

"Painting represents one of the last ruses of the human being by which to express oneself without naming, simply by showing, evoking imaginary or distant scenes, like children who dream every night that they are eating because they have had to go to bed fasting, and who awake hungry because bread is expensive and life is harsh."

Never wallowing in misery, this permanent hymn to life and its mysteries is not simply a matter for painters: it is the genius of a whole people. The *tap-taps*, common transportation of the poor, christened and brightly colored, veritable rolling museums of an art for everyone, reflect the values, the beliefs, the daily life, the condition of the spirit of a whole people: a people that rejects the darkness into which it has been plunged, a people capable of overcoming the vicissitudes of the human condition, a people that today identifies so much with the man whom they themselves have chosen.

— CHRISTOPHE WARGNY

NOTES

1. *Le Nouvelliste,* a Haitian daily paper, February 1991.
2. This was a movement of revenge on the part of the majority blacks against the influence of the mulatto minority.

II

Itinerary

CHAPTER 3

A People
That Does Not
Give Up

Never will I forget that night of December 16! It was December 16, 1990, an almost cool evening in the Caribbean winter: an electric evening, even if the electricity, like so many other things in Haiti, was often lacking. In fact, it was an evening glowing with the hope and the fervor of a whole people.

Even if we did not really doubt it, we waited. We awaited the results of the first free election in our history. All day long Haitians had been voting in overwhelming numbers. How many people had whispered or shouted it to me: dodging bullets, skimming over walls, on all fours or with heads held high—"we are going to vote." Even if the candidate is called Titid, his affectionate nickname, the people had for the first time the feeling of voting for themselves, for their own demands, for their own vision of the world. From the springs of many organizations, from an infinite number of rivulets had been born this torrent, *"lavalas"* in Creole, that would sweep away the loathsome debris of successive dictatorships.

At times there were thousands waiting to vote on the borders of the slums, standing in line, sometimes in whole families, with patience and beauty. Beauty? Indeed, because even at the worst times the Haitian people have cultivated this sense with zeal and extraordinary perseverance. Sometimes they waited for hours in the blazing sun, all my illiterate brothers and sisters, outside their miserable huts. They waited as long as necessary, armed with their little cards marked "NS," the mark for the *Lavalas* list, colored as red as a prize rooster. Even in the residential districts of Pétionville, several kilometers outside Port-au-Prince, farther from the unhealthful miasmas of the central city, we were winning. The immeasurable crowds that had gathered throughout the campaign were witnesses. Never in the memory of black people had anyone seen sixty thousand people at Cap Haïtien, the second-largest city, in the north of the country.

There was hope in their faces, and success was flashing forth every moment, from the bottom of the ballot boxes. Still, for five years, from Namphy to Avril, the generals assisted by the Tontons Macoute and corrupt politicians had again and again stolen the popular victories: by delaying elections or massacring the voters. They had clothed themselves in the garments of democracy in order to laugh at international opinion, while wielding the machete or the revolver against genuine democrats. They spoke of elections, but whispered that an illiterate nation did not have the necessary maturity to vote. And yet there had never been a genuine literacy campaign or even an attempt at schooling: only one child in three ever goes to school. The vicious circle of ignorance and oppression could perpetuate itself *ad vitam aeternam*!

But this time the balloting took place without a major incident, and the hundreds of international observers and dozens of journalists appeared to be armed against fraud or intimidation. There was a group of us, friends, who were waiting, imagining what Roger Lafontant, a leader of the Duvalierists, and his associates could be preparing. At eleven o'clock the telephone rang one more time: "We cannot yet proclaim the official results, but the numbers are such that, practically speaking, you have been elected. Elected! The journalists want to see you!"

It was impossible to arrange a meeting there, where I was, in the middle of the night. It was not until the next morning that I received the delegations of the United Nations and the O.A.S., Bernard Aronson, and the American ambassador Alvin Adams. They confirmed the results for me. "After the party, the drums are heavy," the diplomat whispered to me, jokingly citing a Creole proverb to put me on guard: *"aprè dans, tanbou lou."* I responded, tit for tat, proverb for proverb, *"Men anpil chay pa lou"* ("when there are a lot of hands, the load is not heavy").

A few minutes later, they left. The words we had exchanged in the house were partly drowned out by an enormous noise coming from the city. The decibel level was growing as a spontaneous demonstration of joy suddenly erupted throughout Port-au-Prince. Tens of thousands of Haitians filled the streets around the Champ de Mars at the center of the city. *"Kominike: Titid prezidan,"* chanted the young people climbing on trucks. *Lavalas,* the torrent, flowed noisily around the national palace, to the sound of all the musical instruments that could be quickly assembled. An improvised carnival was stirring up the capital city. For fear that the crowd might run over us in an attempt to congratulate us and hug me, the frail Titid, to death—for we had not had the foresight to put up a barrier—someone quickly thrust me into an auto. It was a strange morning: I had to flee from the human tide I had so often gone out to meet.

And the wave rose and rose with the force of a cyclone. It was a hundred times greater than February 7, 1986. And yet this February 7 what enthusiasm there was, what a memorable day! It had taken fifty-eight months to transform the departure of Jean-Claude Duvalier into the advent of democracy, and I was reduced to listening to the eyewitnesses, to the radio, finally seeing the pictures on television. I was, for the time being, a prisoner: the prisoner of my friends, of my

brothers and sisters, but still, how frustrating! I was missing
the chance to bathe in the human torrent of *Lavalas* shouting
its unmingled joy and its recovered dignity: *"Tout moun se
moun"* ("we are all human beings").

But misfortune is good for everything, especially if the misfortune constitutes such great happiness! Instead of the
immersion that might have drowned me, I had some time to
meditate, to reflect a little on the road we had travelled: a
road of hope and wonderful encounters, but also a road
strewn with corpses, all the victims of that blind and bloody
mafia. Hundreds and thousands of them since 1986 had confronted the groups that prolonged Duvalierism beyond Duvalier. Less than two weeks earlier they had exploded one of
their infernal devices during a meeting at Pétionville. Again,
the bomb had been directed at me. Young people there were
horribly torn to bits.

As on every occasion when I manage to think of the past,
the time machine recalls to me a man who had a particular
impact on my youth: my maternal grandfather. Whatever I
am, influenced by so many admirable women and men, I owe
the most to him.

I was born in Port-Salut, in the southwestern part of the
island, on July 15, 1953. It was not in the heart of the village,
but in a little house among the hills, the *"mornes,"* as we call
the greater part of the country, those cultivated hills where
two-thirds of Haitians live. There are no trees; the deforestation is so great that erosion is progressing rapidly. There
are neither roads, nor water, nor electricity, nor any kind of
farming. Things have scarcely changed in thirty-eight years:
the town always shows the same willingness to change, coun-
tered by the same misery, sister to the same corruption.

My father died shortly after I was born, and my mother,
my sister Anne-Marie, two years older, and I all emigrated
to the capital. But I was to return often to my native district,
to my grandfather's house. As far as we can trace our family

roots, we have all been peasants, but land-owning peasants. Without being in the slightest a "grandee"—one of those speculators who accumulate a huge amount of ill-acquired property—my father had owned more land than the average person. How could my grandfather have been seen as one of those rural gentleman-exploiters of peasant misery, he who shared his life and his lands with others? When I returned to the hills after months of absence I ran up the path to meet him. He was working the land with the others, a land he shared with those who had none. Although he never heard and, consequently, never used the word, he behaved like a socialist.

This respected man played the role of justice of the peace. They brought to his house people who had been arrested, sometimes bearing the marks of blows. Their crime? They had stolen a potato, a banana. That same evening, at the risk of looking bad in the eyes of the oppressors, he would release them, saying: "They took the potato because they were hungry; they have a right to it." My grandfather wanted to be certain that everyone in the hills of Port-Salut ate at least once a day. He knew that the real thieves were not the ones who were brought before him. This humanist was revolted by injustice, whether of birth or of life. I did not have to look far for the sources of my inspiration, the feeling of revolt that began to move me when my conscience was stirred during my adolescence.

The word "justice" was constantly on his lips. My grandfather did not know how to read or write, but he expressed moral and transcendental values better than the greatest books. His love for others shone in his eyes when he let fly at me, while shaving himself in the morning: "You cannot count the hairs in my beard, but you can count the people here who are suffering from injustice."

My grandfather raged against the abuses of the most corrupt section chiefs (officials in charge of the village). He could play that role, since he was so well known by the people, but he was disgusted at the thought of belonging to a group, all too many of whom were characterized by rapacity and arbitrary conduct. He himself had never seen the inside of a school, but he considered teaching to be the antidote to social discrimination, and he sent all his children to school. He was fully aware of the plot hatched by the leaders who were keeping the people weighed down by illiteracy.

He thought that everyone should go to school, but there was an unjust burden laid on my mother. At a very early age she had to play the role of mother, to help my grandfather when he was widowed. Orphans or not, the tradition often shunts older daughters into an auxiliary parental role. They are sacrificed to the family organization.

Every summer I returned to Port-Salut. My grandfather showed me his gardens with great passion, insisting that everyone should work and sacrifice to make the land fruitful: a land that everyone had ardently cultivated and whose fruits everyone, whether an owner or not, could share according to his or her needs.

I would have been scolded if I had not greeted every peasant and every family with equal respect. I ate with them and sometimes slept with their children in their huts. It was as if my grandfather was trying to make me remember at every moment that, no matter how poor, every person is a human being.

I was being schooled by a wise man, who was happy to play with us and even happier to answer his grandchildren's questions. I was certainly too young to always discern the rare quality of that environment. But I believe that in the heart of this family I was infected with the priestly virus — please do not read more than a little malice in that word, for the disease I contracted was nothing but a concern for others.

The hills were for summertime, since my mother very quickly left Port-Salut for the capital, taking her two children with her. There were only the three of us, but we were part of a much larger household: aunts, cousins, friends, country people who for the moment had no place to stay. There were always a dozen or so people sharing the little we had at our disposal. No one gave it a second thought. On Sundays my aunts gathered an even larger group together to talk about God and to conduct religious services. This may appear to be something of an exaggeration, but from country to city I had the feeling of participating in more than family life: it was a communitarian existence, a "socialist" reality on a small scale.

In the summers we returned to Port-Salut, where the sweetness of family life contrasted with the daily struggle conducted by the people there against a land that was so hard and ungrateful, much of the time, to the meticulous care lavished on it. To work these plots required courageous people, those anonymous heroes whom the Haitian people have always produced. There were no draft animals, and only the most rudimentary agricultural implements—nothing but simple hoes—and still less in the way of advice, since the peasants were resistant to it. Organized in groups that mingled a sense of community with egalitarian aspirations, their micro-society possessed, if not the secret of success, at least that of preservation and of hope.

Try to imagine a group of about three dozen. Since they never had clocks or watches, the *lanbi*, or tom-tom, served as a signal to gather the work gangs, the *konbit*. Among them I discovered an organized people, their tools made by those who wielded them, who showed perfect solidarity in their work. It was an egalitarian social organization whose guiding purpose was to furnish the necessary food for each family. Had it not been for the abuses of the local potentates, and sometimes the caprices of the weather, they would have succeeded.

As a child, I found myself in their midst in what was, I admit, a privileged position. I was often regarded as the little prince returned from Port-au-Prince. Living in the capital, a place so distant as to be mythical in their eyes, I may perhaps have appeared to them like a star fallen from the sky. My sister and I took part in the work, certainly, but we also wrote letters for them. Reading and writing were fascinating things in a poor village in the hills, resembling every other village in the hills. I would have liked for them to learn to read and write, too, right away, in the town.

Although they dismissed me as a little prince without the least acrimony or the slightest shade of regret, I could not endure it at the time. Beyond writing their letters or checking their catechism, Anne-Marie and I made several attempts to bring literacy to our friends. It was for us both a duty and a game: we were children, and the joy of life that these rough country people had overcame everything. They had no idea of all that they gave me and would give me. That village of scattered huts, so much like all the others, was my point of reference. There are my roots.

Conversation there revolved around work, daily life and solidarity. I can scarcely recall any frankly political discussions. Our region was perhaps affected less than others by the abuses of the section chiefs. At the beginning, Duvalier was less entrenched there than elsewhere. The most terrible stories, often told in hushed voices, came from beyond our hills. In the hill country of Port-Salut, it may be that the stature of my grandfather preserved us in part from the Macoute devils.

Contrary to the views of certain historians or ethnologists, I saw there a people who never succumbed to resignation. No matter how hard life was, or death, they tried to transform it.

These women and men appeared to me to be so many symbols of goodness. I do not want to slip into some kind of elementary Rousseauism. Certainly there was wickedness there, and quarrels were not rare things. The human being is good within his or her limits and sometimes puts a foot on the bad side — tentatively, always tentatively. In brief, the quintessence of goodness and of the spirit of justice appeared to me to be joined there in a paradise of simple and honest morals.

It was in those hills that the spirit of the people crystallized in its most pure state. Port-au-Prince, in the 1950s, was already a crossroads, a place where opposing currents converged: currents of thought and of action, of justice and of corruption. It was not always easy to find there the simplicity and serenity of the peasant spirit, even if the roots of the people were the same.

As a widow, my mother at first came and went between the capital and Port-Salut. But at the period of my first memories she was settled in Port-au-Prince. We had no fixed residence and I have no shortage of memories of moving. We rented quarters in a wide variety of localities, something that gave me an acquaintance with greatly contrasting places, from the Street of the Caesars, a poor area, to Marcelin Alley, at that time a rich section, now more middle class.

Our lodgings were always more properly a household than a house. We never lived alone, just we three, a mother and two children. We were never less than ten people under one roof: family members, cousins (sometimes quite distantly related), but for the most part friends, peasants from the hill country in search of a roof for the night, a month, or even longer. The house was always full. It was there that I found the sense of, or rather the taste for, community. I feel even today that that brotherhood and sisterhood are something authentically biblical. When Jesus defined his sisters and brothers not as those who came from the womb of his mother, but as his companions, I felt myself molded by those words, immersed in their practice. They were all my brothers and sisters, just as my companions in struggle would later be, both the young intellectuals and the starving people from the slums.

Our family life was not without its lively moments. The passing guests were one element; others included visits to friends, learning music with the aid of the guitar, reading books. These last were two occupations that, separately or simultaneously, would never leave me, two comforts in the darkest hours at a later day.

My mother kept the pot boiling, with a lot of courage, imagination and talent. She bought and sold, moving from one business to another according to the economic conditions, modifying her strategies in response to the needs and opportunities of the moment. All that was done, of course, at the craft level. She had not the least share in the "capitalist" spirit—her meager profits served primarily to feed the whole tribe of us—but she had a lot of creativity and an inventive spirit. Our house, at the crossroads of various distribution routes, sometimes had the air of a commercial establishment. People were there to exchange merchandise— cloth, for example. But perhaps because I have little taste for commercialism or for marketing, my memories of all that are rather vague.

Which of us, in retrospect, does not remember his or her first day at school? When I was five years old, I began school with the Salesian brothers. I had certainly heard people speaking French, especially on the radio, but I spoke only the common language, Creole. That language, however, was formally forbidden by our teachers.

We were to speak nothing but French, even among ourselves. Punishments rained on those who transgressed. Those who "forgot themselves" and spoke aloud in Creole were given a little piece of wood, the symbol of their mistake. One could not get rid of that object except by passing it on to the next person who forgot and spoke in Creole. At the end of the day, the unlucky one whose hand was holding that symbolic object polished by so many fingers was punished and beaten in front of the other students. The teacher often demonstrated even greater malice. He could, at any hour of the day, ask who was holding the "donkey cap," and thus repeat the blows and punishments many times during a single day.

The requirement that we speak French did not really shock us. We were happy to speak the language of Pascal, not because it was forced on us, but because we sensed the necessity of knowing it and practicing it. The taste for knowledge and the thirst for learning prevailed over the injustice of the constraint. We often spoke French with our comrades outside of school, and we even met voluntarily to practice and perfect the language.

Much later came the feeling of revolt against that injustice inflicted on the Haitian nation. To forbid someone to speak his or her own language, to require a people to be ashamed of its own speech! For some people, the difficulty of learning French is partly political or psychological: they cannot command that language because in their minds it is synonymous first with slavery, and then with linguistic servitude. Since the French had been chased out, what was the point of giving a privileged place to their language and abandoning our own? The necessary harmony between the two languages can only occur in the form of a recovered freedom, an elimination of the consequences of the past.

There were about fifty of us in the class, and the Fathers, our teachers, were seldom Haitians, but primarily French, Belgians, or Italians. They were very demanding, especially of the better students. I may say without false modesty that I was one of these.

In Preparatory II, I belonged to the little group of those at the head of the class. If I did not have the best grade I was beaten, just as others were punished for not coming up to the average. They had decided that I ought to be first. And even when I was first, if my average fell below 80 percent I was beaten. When the majority left ten mistakes lying around in their dictation and I made only three—three mistakes meant three blows with the rod!

Why did I receive this favored treatment? I could be accused of a lack of humility, but I was judged to be a brilliant scholar, and the teachers thought it normal to ask more and better things of me at all times. I think they already saw me as a future priest.

Don't think that school was hell. The good moments were just as frequent. I remember playing ping-pong and soccer. The round ball was a great friend of mine; I had begun playing when I was five or six and I have never really given it up, even if I am a little short of time nowadays. As goalkeeper or center forward I was a two-footed kicker. When I was older I even played in the Sylvio-Cator stadium, the main sports arena of Port-au-Prince, with my fellow students.

The Fathers pushed me to the presidency of the school clubs, such as the Dominic Savio Club and the Don Bosco Club. This had some advantages. I loved discussions, holding debates, and arguing. My sister often remembers that, even as a child, I was frequently the guiding spirit and leader of the group, either because I liked it or because it was the best way to get things done. Obstinate! She claims—and here I leave the responsibility to her—that the leader was apparent even in the child and that the course of my life has never really surprised her.

But, as I understood better later on, the greatest privilege was simply that of going to school, something that only 15 percent of the children did on a regular basis. This figure has scarcely changed in thirty years: literacy campaigns have always been shameless hoaxes!

I remained with the Salesian Fathers—men who were both priests and educators—until I was fourteen. It was a traditional and sometimes rough pedagogy, but there was a great deal of affection between teachers and students. God was a God of love. They attempted to prepare us for lives as Christians and as citizens. Even if their vision of solidarity was accompanied by a paternalism that was not subject to discussion, the education they offered was not limited to intellectual knowledge, but was open to the surrounding milieu.

Political or social allusions were never direct, but *sotto voce*. Obliging the dictatorship, the Fathers denounced the *borlette* or lottery, and all games of chance, for their immorality, but also because they masked deeper injustices. "Lord Jesus, deliver us from the *cyclone borlette!*" The name of Duvalier was not spoken, but they called from the pulpit for a movement toward the solution of social problems, generalizing these in terms of the lottery. To speak of misery when the Duvaliers were describing Haiti as the best of all worlds was to take risks. Fathers Désir, Simon, Volel, and undoubtedly others were threatened for raising their voices.

One day the Macoutes set fire to the populous quarter of La Saline, simply because speculators associated with Duvalier wanted to take possession of the land. The people arrived, laden with the bundles of their personal effects that they had been able to salvage, at the Salesians' door. We had to drive them to Cité-Soleil. Madame Adolphe, a *fillette lalo* (a "daughter of the law") — a female Macoute and one of the worst of them — was distributing sheets of tin. For the first time I had a sense of the paroxysm of their imposture: the Macoutes set fire to the peoples' houses and then put themselves in the role of benefactors by handing out a few pieces of corrugated tin. Together with Father Volel, I helped the people to build what no one in any other country would dare to call a house. For me, this was not the moment of discovering the most impoverished people, but the first concrete action performed for them.

It sometimes happened, either in Port-au-Prince or in my native village, that people discussed politics. The opposition was timid, even though a few old people announced frankly that they hated Duvalier. At the age of nine or ten, I began to detest the dictator I did not know. Perhaps unconsciously, my sister, who studied with the Salesian sisters, and I turned away when Duvalier spoke on the radio and lowered our heads when our eyes encountered his picture, which was on posters almost everywhere. We ourselves had nothing in particular to complain about: our family lived comfortably and none of our close relatives had ever been taken to Fort Dimanche, the center for the torture and liquidation of political prisoners.

We talked about God more than we did about politics. At home we read from the Bible and, before a tiny altar, we repeated together the services we had learned from the Salesian priests or sisters. Was this a flight from politics or a means of addressing the subject theologically? It is God's will that we share with the poor. It is God's will that children should love and help their friends. These simple lessons drew me toward those who were hungry, with whom I could share. Here was a theological strength that allowed me to grow up without being totally crushed by the silence of the dictatorship.

But even for a child the system was only too evident. The school run by the Salesian priests was not very far from Fort Dimanche. People were arrested right on the street and mistreated. Sometimes we ran across the Macoutes pushing people covered with blood toward the sinister prison at the ocean's edge. We were not surprised to hear the names of people who had disappeared. The radio itself disseminated the songs of François Duvalier: *"Mache pran yo"* ("Take them!") — no matter who, no matter when. Even a child of ten or twelve, protected by its mother, could not avoid sensing the death that lurked everywhere.

The violence being done to the Haitian people may have determined my priestly vocation. My choice had ripened long before 1966, when I finished primary school. My desire to enter the seminary did not surprise anyone: neither my mother nor my sister, nor my friends, nor the Salesian Fathers. As I have already said, the priestly virus had bitten me at a very early age. I saw my aunts organizing religious celebrations; I admired my grandfather for living and defending human rights every day, and my mother providing by her self-sacrifice for the needs of the household. I myself had also cultivated a taste for service, for saying to others: "I am here for you." My vocation became more and more clear.

Every child is tempted to imitate or reproduce its parental models. But no one in our family was a priest and, although some were very devout, no one in the Aristide family pushed me toward the priesthood. In my very deepest memories I can find nothing but a natural bent, a need, and a certainty that grew stronger and stronger.

My mother, who sensed my vocation, was happy about it. She anticipated my decision, already seeing me as a priest before I had said a word about it. She had done so much for our education, refusing any remarriage for fear that a stepfather would not love Anne-Marie and Jean-Bertrand enough; she was so demanding of herself and others, so good to everyone, feeling a genuine happiness about it. This was one of the better moments in an existence of total devotion. She, who could easily have made a "fine match," as we say, because her family had some property at Port-Salut, had always told me: "I prefer to live in poverty and give you a good education rather than to risk an adventure with someone or other; your affection and your future come first."

Becoming a priest could be seen as a free gift of God or as a social promotion. It is possible that some members of the family were proud, on the basis of the second hypothesis, but I never really felt it. For me, family life was an anticipation of service in the community, banishing the image of promotion and replacing it with that of sharing. I only wanted to go on serving.

I scarcely knew any priests except the Salesians; I had little contact with those in the parishes, where the distance between those who celebrated and those who were in attendance at Sunday Mass appeared to me to be very great. With the Salesians we were comrades, and we lived like fathers, sons and brothers. There was a rapport that was friendly, fraternal, and familial, and a feeling of sharing throughout every day the things that were most true. In short, it was a very Christian reality in the biblical sense.

I entered the Salesian seminary at Cap Haïtien in 1966. Undoubtedly, I had a feeling of moving toward an objective I hoped to attain, but even more there was a feeling of continuity. I was on a journey together with my good companions, in an atmosphere which in no way smacked of exclusion or distancing, even though, since we were three kilometers from the city, we went out very little during the first year. From soccer to orchestral music, creativity was everywhere: in sports, in culture, in religion.

From the seminary we went to the Notre Dame secondary school, where we could receive our friends: the life there was like that in a *lycée*, with only one (sizeable!) difference: we were preparing for the priestly life. What did that mean? There were conferences, Mass every evening, the director's daily talk, "the evening word," which, either encouraging or critical, completed our formation. In short, it was a family life shared by about twenty or thirty Haitian novices. Even today, on the screen of memory I can find no images of anything like regret.

I remember the wonderful summer camps where we slept on the beach and spent two or three uninterrupted hours a day swimming. These emotions, these memories remain vivid, as does the background against which they made their impression: the great number of poor people encountered in the street, with whom I shared a little food and the inexorable human condition.

As I passed from one school to the next, I remained first in the class. My reputation as a clever student gave me a natural authority, which I may have abused, for example, by placing myself too often at the head of different groups. These might be for academics or for sports: I was captain of the soccer team, patrol leader in the Scouts (my patrol was called "Rooster"), leader of the orchestra. It was there that I wrote my first songs before setting them to music.

The subject of charity occupied a primary place in our education. When we thought of "the poor," we were more inclined to imagine starving vagabonds than outsiders who have lost everything but their dignity—although these latter make up the majority of Haitians. The Salesians are particularly sensitive to poverty, since John Bosco chose to help the poorest youth. Our formation gravitated around one axis: to encounter and serve the poor. The definitions did not always coincide fully with my own ideas, the outgrowth of my family life and of the community formation received there.

Vatican II had its impact especially on priestly formation: what a priest should be, what the church is, respect for authority. Fidelity to the Pope and the reality of the Catholic church were reinforced by Salesian formation, since John Bosco had cultivated a special affection for the sovereign pontiff. Politics did not penetrate the seminary. There were certain taboo words that I rarely heard used: communist, for example. Or they were used only to describe the devil. This in no way meant that the Salesians flattered the regime. When Duvalier had some young people from the Cap thrown into prison and quickly accused them of communism, and when the police sweeps became repeated, blind and violent, our director, Father Simon, redoubled his efforts and obtained their liberation. Without ever making a frontal attack on the dictatorship or the forces of national security, he adopted a posture of partisan neutrality. He considered it his duty to meddle in the place where he was.

I began, or continued, at the seminary to satisfy my insatiable appetite for foreign languages. This was something that required scarcely any effort on my part. After learning French, Latin, and Greek, I began to study English and Spanish. Then I learned Italian on my own, since my sister was studying in Italy. That was in 1969. I bought some books and even asked Anne-Marie to write to me in the Roman language. This taste for languages, about which I have often been asked, is nothing but an extension of my love for others: quite simply, it represents a desire to understand them better. I cannot conceive my life in any way but as filled by others. I must have other people beside me. Even more: I need for them to be within me. Communion with others means entering into them in their totality. Communion is communication. Learning a language means establishing a direct contact with others. I feel myself to be Haitian to the depths of my being, but I need a better understanding of other cultures in order that I may respect them more.

It is true that I am fascinated by the "other." I had this fascination when I left the seminary, even before I began to study psychology (which means understanding the other), and it challenges me even today with the same voracious and penetrating power. As for theology, speaking of God and of other people is often a synthesis.

I have surely been lacking at times in modesty or in discernment. If learning languages means understanding others' culture, I asked myself what use Latin was to me, even though I thought I had mastered it. Taking my best pen, I then wrote in Latin to the prefect of studies, Father Bédot, to ask him to dispense me from those courses. He replied in the same tongue: "I deeply regret. . . ." I had to go on.

What exasperated me about Latin was not simply the fact that it was a dead language, but the way in which it was used to disrupt communication. The Latin Mass seemed to me the equivalent of the French histrionics of the politicians. In both cases, one thing was certain: no one understood it. Why impose a language that no one—or scarcely anyone—could understand? In French, it was possible to fool the listeners quite easily; or rather, one might speak only for those who could understand, as if the others did not exist. Is the true society the one that understands French? The high-sounding and incomprehensible words push the majority a little deeper into their complex of illiteracy. Those politicians and church people make me think of the "Monsieur Jourdains" or the "*Précieuses ridicules*" of politics—or of religion.

At eighteen I felt myself equally a Haitian and a citizen of the world. I never felt obliged to love men and women because God had ordered me to do so. I was part of the other: in each person I discovered a little of myself, and in myself I found a little of the other. The human being is, at one and the same time, unique and plural.

I took delight in discovering people in books. In Port-au-Prince, the lives of the saints and French literature had an essential place, and we were encouraged to read. Pascal and Jean-Jacques Rousseau left their mark on me, but I was passionately fond of everything written, especially books. Today, just like twenty years ago, I cannot make my way through all the books that occupy my room; you will find them on my bed as, in someone else's room, you would expect to find pillows. It sometimes happens that I awaken uncomfortably during the night: the corner of a solid binding is digging into my shoulder!

At the beginning of the 1970s, South American literature took on the greatest importance. It quickly articulated for itself a philosophy and a theology: here, the antagonism between exploiter and exploited became more and more clear as I pursued my reading. When I speak of South American literature I am thinking also of Caribbean works, and certainly those of Haiti: *Le Gouverneur de la rosée* by Jacques Roumain, or *Compère général soleil* by Jacques Stephen Alexis were the masterpieces. In them, as in my encounter with the great Haitian poets like Etzer Vilaire or Oswald Durand, I found an atmosphere that allowed me to understand and to be reborn.

After leaving the seminary I devoted more time to philosophers and theologians. The thought of Gabriel Marcel, who affirmed that the human being is his or her body and soul, responded to my theological vision, which was itself enlightened by Leonardo Boff, Rudy Erès, and so many other Americans. When I think of Plato and Aristotle, required subjects in secondary school, I do not regret having studied them, but I find myself very critical of them.

As for the Bible, I have read it through thirty-some times. The first reading is mixed up in my mind with learning to read. I return to it always in response to a thought, or a search, and I am engulfed by it. It is as if each time I am reading it for the first time. I even take pleasure in comparing translations, especially since my period of residence in Israel. With each translation a new approach is born.

CHAPTER 4

Fascination
with Other Cultures

I finished the seminary when I was twenty-one, and left Haiti for the first time, though without leaving the island. The place chosen by the Salesians for their novitiate is ordinarily in the Dominican Republic. The novitiate is a year during which the novice takes his or her first vows, after a period of formation in accord with the particular spirituality of the congregation.

One year later I returned to Haiti and entered the state university in Port-au-Prince to study philosophy and psychology: the former in the morning, the latter in the afternoon. What pleasure it gave me, and what a game it was to articulate the complementarity of these two forms of thought! The congregation provided for my needs, and I was a genuine student among others. The majority of them came from the middle classes, the upper bourgeoisie preferring to send their children abroad to institutions that were better equipped and more prestigious. Many were there only at the cost of heavy sacrifices on their own part or that of their families. The regime kept a close eye on the university, which it viewed as a highly risky place for it, but there we breathed a little bit of the foretaste of democracy.

I received my degree in psychology in 1979. The end of

the 1970s coincided with a more and more active militancy. Radios, as numerous as today and more and more listened to, played a dominant role in raising consciousness. I was responsible for the programming at Radio Cacique. I had already made a mark with my musical compositions; this was a different mode of expression but one with a more immediate impact.

Commentaries on the Bible, quotes from the Bible itself, imagery, stage pieces, short plays — the tone of the broadcasts was varied and independent, to the extent possible under Jean-Claude Duvalier. Thus on one occasion I needed two young people. My car was broken down. Three of us rode one motorcycle, riding in total darkness. We were in extremis when we arrived at the station at five o'clock in the morning. We really made do with what we had. A brief scene had to be played between a poor person and a traveller who had arrived from England. "The European," a bourgeois, made fun of the poor person stagnating in a pitiful daily existence. The exercise was a little didactic: it consisted in dramatizing a reality in order to speed up the raising of social consciousness, X-raying Haitian society, and setting to music the realities of our country.

My imagination was fertile at that period, and I took a lot of pleasure in it. The profession of journalist and commentator had always exercised a certain attraction for me. Commentator, preacher — is there such a great difference between the two?

The director of the station — a good director — was sometimes uneasy. "Uneasy" is a euphemism. He certainly carried on under heavy pressure. He made repeated and strong signals to encourage me to abbreviate or change the subject. I sometimes complied, but slyly. I would drop my commentary only to quote texts from the Bible that were even more impertinent and accusatory than the commentaries themselves. The gospel in its raw form could act like a stick of dynamite. The director sometimes interrupted the broadcast abruptly and completely changed the subject, to the great disadvantage of the listeners.

The two years of 1979 and 1980 marked a turning-point in the struggle against Jean-Claude Duvalier in Haiti, and coincided with the meeting of the Latin American bishops' conference in Puebla, Mexico. The difficult confrontations I had with the radio programs were repeated at the church and within the church. How many times in those years did I get my ears boxed by my pastor after I had expressed my opinions in public: "You are going too fast. If you don't slow down, you will run the risk of getting us all arrested. What you are saying is political, and the church should not be involved in politics." My director, Bishop Kebreau, leaned toward me and whispered in my ear: "Don't go driving two hundred miles an hour: fifty is fast enough."

After 1975 I could not help stating my position vis-à-vis the traditional church: giving priority to the poor. A few years later, my choices had become definitive and radical, as was my conviction that the majority of our church had decided, if not to compromise with power, at least to be silent, and even to preach resignation. Ten or fifteen years later, my opinion has not changed.

There were some priests who were openly on the side of the Macoutes. There were also some bad priests who accepted everything and who happily joined in social sin and in collaboration. They pointed out the poor sinners, those who stole bananas or were unfaithful to their spouses, while closing their eyes to the overall structures of corruption. They inveighed against trifles and made a covenant with the devil.

Consciously or not, they placed the authority of the church in the service of evil. Perhaps we should give a more nuanced judgment: they were often victims of their own formation. The Catholic church, with its rigid structures, prepared individuals (priests, and male and female religious) to function in the traditional — machinelike — manner. Preservation was more important than the gospel. Inside, in spite of the power of the system, a small group of priests resisted the Pharisees who held the reins of command. It was a group whose numbers were steadily growing and whose audience was growing even faster. These were priests who resisted the rigidity, the degradation, and the ultimate fossilization, and who were demanding an opening of the doors and windows. Those who were hand in glove with Macoutism made up an easily identifiable minority. They had long since chosen their side. The majority were prudent and timid; they hesitated. It was a somnolent swamp. The arrival of Father Godeffroy Midi in 1977 played an essential role. He was a saintly man, humble, simple, good, someone who understood how to transform prophecy and put it into action. There are a number of us who owe a great deal to him.

We used to meet in the late 1970s, not entirely secretly, like children who hide out in order to commit little acts of mischief, but trying not to attract too much attention from the hierarchy. I had already been "burned" a few times. Perhaps it was hoped that I would leave the country to continue my theological studies somewhere else, in Israel for example. The archbishop of Port-au-Prince, Monsignor François-Wolff Ligondé, had no hesitation in exiling confrères whose sermons echoed the voices of the poor by sending them into the hill country.

Archbishop Ligondé, consecrated during the 1960s, had banished the Jesuits and the Spiritan Fathers, the latter having tried to make the words of Christ a reality in Haiti. I take no pleasure in recalling recent memories, but the archbishop of Port-au-Prince demonstrated, up to the time of his flight in 1991, that he was a zealous servant of Macoutism.

In January 1985, after my return, I met Archbishop Ligondé a number of times. He asked me to translate the Bible into Creole. As for dialogue between us, I concealed nothing from him concerning my theological thinking or my opinion of the Haitian church. I certainly would not have convinced him. At any rate, he preferred to close his door and to address his messages to me through the mediation of my Salesian superiors—before turning the matter over directly to the Macoute mercenaries.

At that time, bishops and Macoutes walked arm in arm, defending the same causes, but using a different vocabulary to mask their collusion for the benefit of the oligarchy, the banking bourgeoisie without ideals or principles whose profits were invested outside Haiti.

In that summer of 1979 the provincial of the Salesians (for the Caribbean province), while visiting Port-au-Prince, suggested to me that I should leave. The quality of my grades at the university, where I had received 90 out of a possible 100 points for my thesis in psychology, had earned me a trip to Rome — or rather, a stop there en route, since Father Enrique Mellano was proposing that I should go to Israel for biblical studies.

Was the purpose to get me out of Haiti or to bring me back to a sober reading of the Bible? Did my superiors see me as a future seminary professor, on condition that I accommodate myself to the norm? Or was it some kind of recompense? The Salesian superiors and the Macoute bishops were not pursuing the same ends, but I think that, for different and even opposite reasons, both of them wanted to see me leave for Jerusalem.

I remember a professor of biblical studies to whom I had presented one of my poetic works. In *Pou ki* I retold Genesis in the form of Creole poetry. He thought it should be published. From that moment on, it was thought that I showed great interest in biblical studies. My good knowledge of theology combined with my capacity to learn new languages might make a biblical scholar of me. This proposal would let me cultivate archeological, linguistic, and biblical research.

The Salesians hoped to turn me into a learned priest, a great professor. They sincerely loved me. At that time, Ligondé did not have so much influence over the community that he could have ordered my departure as a punishment — something that he never failed to do in the cases of rebellious diocesan priests. The Salesians pictured me having a fine career, once the impetuosity of youth had dissipated. They were right in their own way: they were wrong only about the course the journey would take. One of them said to me later, when I was giving a course in Hebrew: "It seems as if you have not given proper attention to your episcopal career!" No doubt he was right. If I had mixed a lot of water in my wine, I might one day have been made a bishop. Think of it: Jean-Bertrand Aristide, a colleague of François-Wolff Ligondé!

I left to meet Israel and the land of Christ. I also made the acquaintance of Palestine, and the violent clashes between the two communities there. Without pretending to be naive or retreating into a false neutrality, I can say that I love these two peoples passionately. I had friends in both camps. Jews, Muslims, Christians: the differences of religion meant little to me. For years I had learned in Haiti to judge human beings not by their religion, but by what they are and by what they do, by the correspondence between "saying" and "being."

Jews and Palestinians suffered under the same forces of oppression as we Haitians: racism and colonialism. I sensed the common denominator among the three peoples. How can we identify the oppressors without turning them against us? How can we respond to violence with nonviolence? These questions could be asked just as well in Port-au-Prince as in Jerusalem.

My desire to understand others' culture sometimes became an obsession: "Why do they dance? Why do they stick those little bits of paper into the Wailing Wall? Why . . .?" I felt myself still more fascinated by people, wherever they were, whatever they were. That is why I have such a hard time accepting it when other people reject my culture or violate my rights. I am as jealous for the rights of others as for my own. In Haiti when I heard a priest, a Frenchman, in the name of his faith, reprimand the peasants and denounce voodoo celebrations as a garbage can of superstitions, I felt revolt growing within me. I rejected what he was saying; to me it seemed like robbery.

In Israel, as in Haiti, I felt myself to be at the center of history. History, that essential discipline which held a prime place in the seminary, is made to be lived from within. It is like theology in that sense: I have never been able to live it any other way. I have a hard time understanding a place apart from its history, and when I think of it, I find myself once more embedded in history. How can there be two histories, one sacred and the other profane? I am more convinced than ever that there is only one history: that of human beings, that which helps us to explain the struggle for humanity.

I plunged into the study of Hebrew and Arabic. It was too bad that I had to neglect the latter in favor of the language of the Jews, which was indispensable for my biblical studies. I lived in Bethlehem, but I traveled to Jerusalem nearly every day to take intensive courses in Hebrew. I was learning the language of a people whose roots went back two thousand years. What greater thing could be hoped for by someone who was passionately interested in different cultures?

Three years later, I finished my biblical studies, needing only a few more months to complete my doctoral dissertation in theology. In June 1982 I returned to Port-au-Prince, even though it had been suggested that I should remain for one more year.

Now, at the age of twenty-five, I wanted to be ordained priest—but not by just any bishop. In my eyes, there was only one bishop among the nine members of the Haitian episcopal conference who seemed truly "acceptable." He was a man who was struggling along with his people: Monsignor Romélus, bishop of Jérémie. The familial ties that connected me with him facilitated matters. I finally negotiated my priestly ordination in exchange for a new exile, in Jerusalem or elsewhere.

If I had been able to remain in Haiti, I would certainly not have left. The student I was, and whom others wished to keep as such, was nevertheless ordained to the priesthood by Bishop Romélus on July 3, 1982. Appointed to the parish of

St. Joseph in Port-au-Prince along with my friend Arthur Volel, I was well aware that it was a precarious mission, and highly provisional! Those were three months that would have weighty consequences.

The Salesians were very fond of me, but the provincial delegate was summoned by the agents of the dictatorship: law and order require that Aristide leave! Lafontant, Estimé and company order it! Did the future Bishop Kebreau have a choice? There was no more question of Jerusalem; I was to go to Canada. They sent me to a pastoral institute that specialized in theological reprogramming. I presented myself to the superior in Montreal bearing a sealed letter (a warrant for my imprisonment) whose contents I did not know. It was a strange journey into the unknown.

The secret of the letter was revealed to me on my arrival: I had been sent there for pastoral reorientation. The superior of the institute had a hard time understanding it: he asked me, "Have you come here to teach?" I had a hard time understanding it myself—or perhaps I understood all too well. They had sent me there to be "reprogrammed." It seemed to him, in view of my academic degrees, that I could not be anything but a teacher. He had no need for me, and preferred to see me go somewhere else.

"You are at the highest academic level, but we have no need of a professor. Instead, you may continue your studies in psychology at the University of Montreal." I had always been passionately fond of psychology, so I started a doctorate.

Quebec seemed to me to be a society of very obvious social classes. National antagonisms played a major role, and this was sometimes translated into a feeling of superiority toward blacks. Being a Christian and a priest made the dialogue easier for me, but the society was full of racial tension.

The Catholic church was in a genuine state of collapse: there were no young people at Mass, and only a few old people. Meanwhile, the church basements were converted into bingo halls overflowing with people! I thought of my teacher's denunciations of the immorality of the lottery.

Here, the *cyclone borlette* had almost replaced the eucharist, and within the very temple itself.

I had no need to visit Quebec to know that a church divorced from its own times, a church that agrees to support oppression, condemns itself. The Quebecois were determined to no longer remain second-class citizens vis-à-vis the Anglophone entrepreneurs and politicians. They intended also to lay claim to their dignity and their language. There is a coincidental, but obvious, paradox here: their second-class language — their Creole — was French.

The church had succeeded in giving indigestion to the whole society. The sacred words (Christ, tabernacle, eucharist) had become, for the most part, swear words, since the institution was regarded as utterly unbearable by all the forces tending toward progress and emancipation. In that society, the church had finally succeeded in killing God. Without the prophetic irruption of the excluded, Haiti might see the same end.

In 1985 I completed my master's degree in biblical theology as well as the course work for a doctorate in psychology. I had chosen to study Old Testament neurosis. In doing so, I took full advantage of the opportunity to read Freud and to deepen my knowledge of liberation theology.

I also encountered some Haitian exiles, including Karl Lévêque, a Jesuit who had been living outside the country for some time and who was killed accidentally, probably assassinated. I got a better idea of the ways in which the Duvalierist oppression extended itself even into the diaspora, beyond Haiti's borders. Those who hoped for the return of a subdued priest were going to change their tune very quickly.

After a study tour in Greece, I returned to Haiti on January 5, 1985, to a country in a state of general mobilization for change.

CHAPTER 5

So Are There Two Gods?

In six years I had spent only a few months in Haiti. Nearly six years of exile! In fact, never at any moment did I have the feeling of having left the country. Even when there was a time difference of six hours between me and Port-au-Prince, I never had the courage to set my watch to Jerusalem time. The study of the Bible, for a student coming from a country of poor and oppressed people, was a steady reminder of them. The Bible, more than ever a message of liberation, proclaimed liberty for those who are deprived of it.

Even when communications were sometimes slow because of the climate of war in the Middle East, I never ceased to write on behalf of Haiti. Father Joris Cueppens published my thoughts, my texts. I contributed, in particular, to the paper *Bon nouvel*. In fact, there were many who thought that some of my barbs would prevent me from ever returning to Haiti.

The four months in the middle of 1982 were decisive. After being ordained priest, I was sent to the parish of St. Joseph, in a poor section. When they heard my sermons, the episcopal authorities, who may have still hoped that ordination would make a choirboy of me, had to sing another tune, and quickly—even though the actual audience was enchanted with the good news.

Between two journeys, I was journeying again: to the interior of a neighborhood, to the country of sub-humanity, of oppression turned to misery or of misery turned to oppression — so much so that some of the images of that dark country seem to lead one to the center of hell. Even if, from time to time, photographs of the slums and their starving people travel throughout the world, it is necessary to see them, to enter the hovels of Port-au-Prince and the network of little streets so narrow that one must often turn sideways, taking care not to step on the children. The sheet-metal huts cannot resist very long against the tropical downpours and the flow of water through the gutters that can wash everything away. The rare water spigots run for only two hours a day, and the precious liquid must be paid for. The people are crowded into spaces so small that they have to take turns sleeping. And yet, even here, people are born, they live, they die.

As one might suspect, nothing had changed since I left for Jerusalem. The work that had been sketched at that time needed to be pursued. It is not easy, at the outset, to forge a bond between the priest — a man of letters, a gentleman — and the vagrants. The first step must be to establish a human relationship, which means that one cannot begin by handing out a few coins. In that case, the exchange becomes commercial and mercenary, and begins on an unequal basis. Barriers are erected at the first contact.

We talk about everything; we go out together. If I leave in a car, they come with me. True, they are dirty, but we go together. Little by little, we come to live together. If we are preparing for a party, they take part. They are the actors, and the drama they are playing is their own.

Imagine the dialogues, sometimes improvised, played before an audience of hundreds:

"The Lord be with you. Go in the peace of Christ."

To which a miserable wretch sitting in front of the church replies:

"But who is this priest who has just told me: 'Go in the peace of Christ,' when I am hungry!?'"

"So there are two gods," adds a second, "one for the priests and the rich, and another for the rest of us rotting here outside the church."

Thus the leading thread of a theological idea unrolls, drawing certainly toward a single God, the God of the outsiders, manipulated by the more fortunate to maintain their ancestral domination over the poor. And the church is an accomplice, imposing a message of resignation: accept the world as it is! With the help of the actors, we invert these propositions.

My sermons, if one listens carefully, lead in the same direction. But the essential point is different: that the poor themselves should also be the actors. In a theology of liberation, the poor people themselves should speak for all their brothers and sisters. This pedagogy, this reality makes sisters and brothers of all of us. Outside, little by little, the marginal and the marginalized began to regard us — even though there had certainly been other priests at the cutting edge long before me — as their spokespersons.

We were forging an almost organic solidarity within the city of oppression. Out of this sharing sprang a question that the authorities found intolerable: "Can we continue to view as normal the violence imposed on the poor?"

My two and a half years in Quebec had changed nothing. It was necessary to break the cycle of misery. The cross of Jesus Christ is a cross of liberation. I knew very well that I would be accused of "being involved in politics," as they say, but liberation takes place through battle against those who are responsible for the destitution and indignity. It is really necessary to put an end to this parasitic regime. "*Bourik travay, chwal galonnen*" ("Pain for some, a party for others").

Macoutism could only survive by means of permanent violence and repression. The Duvaliers could kill anyone, anywhere, anytime. The terror was accompanied by a pillaging of the state treasury by a mafia headed by the Duvalier family.

The oligarchy and the Macoutes had put together a political and economic alliance. Armed force protected their local and international economic interests. The profits of the oligarchy helped to finance their mafia. To perpetuate itself, the system obeyed a single imperative: preserve power. For corruption and barbarism, Haiti, the poorest country in the Americas, broke all records.

How many were auxiliary supporters of the system, often uprooted poor people who never received anything substantial from the millions of dollars that were diverted? There may have been thirty thousand, rebaptized by Jean-Claude Duvalier as "volunteers for national security." Armed with machetes or guns, outfitted with a mixture of equipment, they sowed unlimited terror. These section chiefs, ex-criminals, renegade police, could just as easily use their power to eliminate political opponents or to satisfy personal vendettas. They were all equally thieves, rapists, informers, stoolpigeons, torturers—in a word, assassins. Perhaps not all of them had blood on their hands, but all shared in the responsibility for the thousands of executions carried out at Fort Dimanche and elsewhere. Torture was also practiced at the Dessalines barracks. Although a minority, women also played a part: they were called *"fillettes lalo"* ("daughters of the law").

Even more than the mercenaries, it was the quasi-scientific organizers of this terror that we had to denounce: the barons of Duvalierism, certain sections of the army, of the upper bourgeoisie, and the Macoute priests. This system had endured for twenty-nine years, but it followed three centuries of armed robbery that began with the colonialists, and continued through imperialism and successive oligarchies. The elites often copied the worst principles of imperialism. As I wrote in a song in 1979: *"Gen gwo kolon, gen ti kolon; gen kolon blan, gen kolon nèg"* ("There are big and little colons, there are white and black colons").

As for the army, its leaders were allied with the regime. There were a few who had been pulling the strings for a long time. To overthrow a government, one made use of the army. To support a candidate, one called on the army, a band of mercenaries within which a few patriots managed to survive. Heroes have made their mark even within this army of corruption, associated, like the Tontons Macoute, with smuggling and drug traffic: yesterday it was Charlemagne Péralte, today there are other officers, patriots and incorruptible people. They are rare. But I have known them.

Meanwhile we, the former slaves, whom the new feudal lords had attempted to restore to their slave status, had never let ourselves be completely subdued, not even at the worst times. From the "maroons" (slaves who escaped from plantations and formed separate communities) to the youth of today, we discover a chain of rebellion opposed to the chains of slavery: two centuries of heroic resistance, in the tradition of Toussaint-Louverture, for liberty and equality, without regard to the color of one's skin. If a white will help us to reconquer our freedom, we say: welcome! Such a person is our brother or sister. If a black locks the chains of our servitude more firmly, let him or her be opposed! We will call for his or her *dechoukaj*.

"Tout moun se moun" ("every person is a human being"): despite an oppressive militarism, an ineffective, hypocritical and corrupt administration, a blind and avaricious minority, a state that is nonexistent or terrorist, Haitians have always sought, within their rural structures, to preserve the equality won with independence. There is an instinctive impulse toward equality on the part of the people, in the face of social structures that are profoundly nonegalitarian. Is this an apparent paradox? In fact, we are taking up the torch of two centuries of struggle against injustice.

One should not imagine that my biblical or psychological "parentheses," in Israel or in Canada, were times when I was preoccupied with anything other than the liberation of the people. I found there, instead, a deepening of my reflection and a set of exciting comparisons. The struggle continued within the country, with so many others, some of whom have paid with their lives. However modest it may be, I have continued to offer my contribution.

In 1983, when visiting Haiti, the Pope had cried out: "Things must change!" From Montreal, I had heard this appeal as a command and an encouragement, for the church and for the country.

On my return, I found the land in a more piteous state than ever. Haiti is one of the poorest countries in the world, with a per capita income of three hundred fifty dollars per year, thirty to fifty times less than in the richest countries of Western Europe and North America. And when one takes into account the monstrous inequalities in our society, the figure falls to one hundred dollars for the peasants, perhaps even less for the slum-dwellers. I am not an economist, but what can anyone do with one hundred dollars? What happens to such a person?

The children are the first victims: infant mortality is one hundred twenty per thousand, and more than half the children are physiologically abnormal, whether because of malnutrition or other scourges. How could they be in good health when we have only one doctor for every twenty thousand people, and almost all the doctors are in the cities? Typhoid, tuberculosis, and AIDS are epidemic. There are so few clinics, just as there are so few schools — and even those are dilapidated, both physically and educationally!

Haiti lies within the American orbit, and even if the presidency of Jimmy Carter gave us a little hope, it did not change the American investors in the assembly shops into patrons. We are, so it seems, number one in the world in the production of baseballs, but wages are rarely more than three dollars per working day.

For economic or political reasons, a million or a million and a half Haitians, perhaps more — the figures are never very reliable in this regard — live abroad: in the Caribbean, in North America. Besides those emigrés who have left freely (which is a euphemism: we ought to say those who were pressured or forced to leave), there are those whom the regime has sold like cattle—or, to put it another way, like black slaves. Jean-Claude Duvalier had regular access every year to a regular gold mine of several million dollars for furnishing a few tens of thousands of cane cutters for the Dominican Republic. Maurice Lemoine has described better than anyone else, in his *Sucre amer* (Paris: Éditions Encre, 1981), the deportation and the inhuman living conditions of these people who are subjected to limitless exploitation. Trade in blacks goes on in the middle of the twentieth century!

"Is there such a thing as an economy in Haiti?" some of our foreign visitors ask themselves, seeing the extent to which the country is dependent on the contributions of emigrés, international aid, and illicit traffic of every sort. It begins with drug dealing, in which the government is entangled with no scruples, and which has continued under Namphy and Avril. But unhealthy as it is, the Haitian economy does exist, necessarily. It is a shattered economy, suffering from chronic ills; a *restavek* economy (children sent out to domestic service by their parents are called *restavek* [= *reste avec*] "stay with"). Our economy is the image of our politics: also *restavek.* Political life is totally subordinated to the local political racket and to the international dictates imposed from outside.

Even so, the economy has two faces, for there is also an economy from below: the product of the unceasing labor of the proletariat and the masses of peasants who enable the population to be fed—poorly. Here, too, we are immersed in a fully feudal state of affairs: three-fourths of the land is owned by four percent of the population. Most of the hill-dwellers have nothing but a miserable patch of ground, a handkerchief, *mouchwa tèt,* on which they work themselves to death for nothing.

Our system is, in Creole, a *"tèt sans ko"* ("a head without a body"), an economy in which the head is overfed and gives no thought to the nourishment of the body, where the vitality is sucked out by a minority that enriches itself by shamefully exploiting the masses. It is worse than feudalism. Slavery exists for those cane cutters who are sold without right or law, for the *restavek*, in the share-cropping system in which the owner takes the better half of the harvest, and for so many others.

What kind of mental health, what sense of solidarity, what life force has been necessary for this people to survive in such hostile conditions! We should have been able to count the annual suicides in thousands, so much have the governments transformed the land into hell. And yet the permanent drama has generated fewer suicides than occur in the developed countries.

The land has been stolen by the "big shots," the lawyers, the state. The need for agrarian reform goes without saying. When John Paul II asserted in Haiti, *"Fòk sa chanje"* ("things must change"), this demand followed from his message. Of course, if I interpret it this way I am immediately branded a communist. "Communist" is a condemnatory epithet, a defamatory accusation that the regime throws in the face of anyone who offers the least opposition. You are labeled a communist: that says everything, there is no appeal from this verdict. You are an enemy of the country, an outlaw, a dog thrown out as prey for public condemnation. Anyone can beat you up—because you are a communist. Obviously, it is more difficult to suggest that the Pope is a militant Marxist, but Aristide or those like him . . .?

As if the economic disaster were not enough, the system of laissez-faire combined with political indifference has brought Haiti to the verge of ecological catastrophe. Widespread deforestation is turning our mountains, little by little, into deserts. When one flies over the island, it is easy to pick out the border of the Dominican Republic. To put it briefly, there are no more trees on the Haitian side. Add to this the pollution of the coasts, the shortage of potable water, and the lack of sanitary systems: all this has turned Haiti into a garbage can.

The mafia cared nothing about underdevelopment. During the 1980s, Haiti did not even make use of the total amount of aid or of loans placed at its disposal by international organizations. What did it matter to the minority rolling in wealth? For those at the helm, and for the oligarchy who represent a tiny portion of the population, the rest of the body social does not exist. They are domestic servants, slaves. On the contrary, their social project consists in keeping the people locked in their ignorance and misery. Jean-Claude Duvalier from time to time threw a few handfuls of *gourdes* to the starving, as one might throw bones to the dogs. The political project consisted in reducing human beings to a sub-human status. Why build clinics for the Haitian people when they themselves can take off for Miami at the smallest scratch?

Slavery, in fact, was everywhere. The regime hardened at the beginning of the 1980s. Repression struck the political activities, the labor unions, the militant members of Catholic Action. But protest did not stop. The petitions multiplied, and so did the tracts and clandestine newspapers. Some non-governmental organizations (NGO) did good work. Becoming conscious of their own exploitation, more easily able to compare their country with others (a boomerang effect facilitated by the exiles), the people lifted up their heads. It seemed as if fear were receding, as if the people's justified terror of the Macoutes was becoming weaker than its justified feeling of revolt.

I do not want to put the Christian communities on a pedestal, but I believe that they furnished a driving influence, in a thousand ways, in the neighborhoods and on the radio. The radio, Radio Soleil and Radio Haiti, became an essential instrument of struggle, which the powerful put a stop to whenever they could. I did not have my own program, but from the time of my return I was very much in demand for interviews, sermons, debates, so that my voice was quite frequently on the airwaves.

But I was a priest. What appointment would I be given? Certainly not to support the revolution, which was the real object of my vows. The provincial delegate had suggested that I should teach biblical theology in the major seminary in Port-au-Prince, a logical appointment for a student who had spent so much time acquiring a deeper knowledge of the Bible. I returned on January 5, 1985, and was to begin my courses on the 9th. Suddenly, the program was changed: "Fine . . . you know . . . that is true, but . . . we were thinking of you as a professor of the Bible, but after all . . . we are obliged . . . you will have to go to Les Cayes." Les Cayes, several hours away, in the southwestern corner of the country!

"But the seminary is expecting me in three days. Why this sudden demand that I should leave for Les Cayes? What will you tell the major seminary that is expecting me?"

We discussed it, Father Kebreau and I. At Les Cayes, a provincial town, I would be in charge of the trade school. We arrived at a compromise. I would teach there and commute each week to the major seminary. I would also be chaplain to the Salesian sisters at Les Cayes. Suggestion, counter-suggestion, compromise — they were very fond of me, but at the same time, they did not trust me. One submits to certain pressures, gets around others. In September, while retaining my teaching post at the major seminary, I was made master of studies at the National School for Arts and Crafts in Port-au-Prince, in the parish of St. Jean Bosco, to which I was delighted to return.

I had no intention of limiting myself to that kind of teaching. In 1985, the struggle for the *dechoukaj* (uprooting) of Jean-Claude Duvalier was entering a decisive phase. Fear was no longer multiplying; demonstration followed demonstration. Since the radio stations were closed, it was necessary to devise other means of communication to distribute information, respond to arrests, and maintain the anti-Jean-Claude climate.

Thanks to the couriers, the block captains and neighborhood leaders, we were able to mobilize thousands of young people in a few hours. The net was tightly woven. We did not neglect the provinces, in a country where communications are difficult and uncertain because of the deplorable state of the roads and even more because of the bands of Macoutes who were still sowing terror everywhere. Everyone made it his or her duty to remain faithful to the statement issued at Jérémie by the Youth Congress: "If a young person is unjustly attacked, all young people are attacked . . . all must express their solidarity."

The national security forces were making arrests with all their might. They arrested anyone, sometimes at random. The Macoutes had no hesitation in killing, as at Gonaïves and elsewhere. The victims were the young people, almost always the young people. Every city youth was suspect, and in a country where the population is so young, the majority of the people, more than ever, were presumed guilty. The harder the repression struck, the more it triggered new vocations. The martyrs increased the tension, the pressure. A visceral solidarity made heroism ordinary.

In my contact with exiles and with the world of North America, Macoutism had begun to appear to me not merely as a perverse system, but as an anachronistic regime, a dictatorship at the end of its rope, one that had exhausted all its resources. The Americans understood it quite well. For them, it was a matter of bringing about the departure of the puppet dictator in order to avoid a social cyclone, of promoting a kind of Duvalierism with a human face, thus accelerating change in order to change as little as possible.

I understood that analysis too well to push, on the other hand, for an acceleration of the revolutionary process. There was a sense that victory was at hand. The most radical, the most experienced, were already asking the question: "How shall we keep them from robbing us of our victory?"

Little by little, it was no longer the departure of Jean-Claude Duvalier that was demanded. His *dechoukaj* would not be enough; it was necessary to take him prisoner so that he would have to settle his accounts. Eight days before he fled, we were afraid that he might leave. The young people immediately dragged me with them to the airport to prevent the big bird from taking off. The crowd remained there all night, but it was only a rumor, or the rehearsal for a scene that would soon be played out.

At Les Cayes, every gathering surpassed the numbers of the previous one. I preached in the large cathedral for three days in a row. The whole town was there, a huge crowd outside the building that was already overflowing: Protestants, Catholics, Freemasons were all jostling one another. The faith that drove us found words applying to all of us. It was communion in the strongest sense of the word.

My new position in Port-au-Prince enabled me to offer leadership and encouragement to all the young people who came to St. Jean Bosco as their church, as a place of justice or as a general locality of liberation: the liberation of our society, and also of our church.

All my being was directed toward these two objectives. I emphasized this during the services on January 31, 1986. My life might have ended there. A Tonton Macoute who had come to assassinate me was disarmed by the faithful at the last moment. It was the first of a long series of murderous attempts against me and against so many militants less fortunate than I who were to pay the price for not having respected the law of silence.

Luckily, the young people spotted him. The gentleman was about to draw his revolver during the eucharistic celebration. His name was Stephan Joseph. They beat him unmercifully after disarming him. This man had been paid to shoot me. If he fulfilled his contract, a passport and visa for leaving the country awaited him. Outside, beyond the barrier, there was a scene that would become classic: the military trucks and Macoutes awaiting their protégé.

Between the church and the surrounding wall, the young people began to chant slogans against the dictatorship. We were living in a state of siege. Did they need any other reason for firing into the crowd? I put myself in the front row, but I was afraid that the people would leave the church and, when they entered the nearby streets, be slaughtered like rabbits. Almost entirely surrounded by Macoutes armed to the teeth, we waited. An old man with a bloodied head came slowly forward. The young people tended to him. He continued on his way toward the left. An impulse pushed me toward him. I wanted to give him a dollar for some good soup to revive him a little.

The military took advantage of those few seconds of absence, in response to a perhaps unfortunate reflex, by beating up the young people who had taken refuge in the church. Beating people was a routine job for the majority of these mercenaries, but this time things did not go so badly as they might have. Still, neither the hierarchy nor the apostolic nuncio, Bishop Romeo, uttered a single word of solidarity or even of simple comfort on this occasion.

The fall of the dictator was one of our most memorable days. Even if the puppet did not rid us of the apprentice sorcerers who pulled the strings, even if we would have preferred to imprison him instead of seeing him flee into a gilded exile, February 7, 1986 was not a day for pessimism. There was no question of hesitating in the face of the popular fervor, or of haggling over our joy. We were happy. I have never seen so much rejoicing in the city where I spent my childhood. Everyone certainly deserved a double ration of rum, the better to dance to the sound of the *rara*, our own musical instruments.

We all took part in it. Some of us knew that we had only reached a certain stage. The symbol of the dictatorship was on its way to join others in the garbage cans of history, but the foundations were not going to disappear from one day to the next. Jean-Claude had departed, but the powers of death remained: his squadrons, his mafia.

CHAPTER 6

Fòk Sa Chanje
(Things Must Change)

A few weeks after the installation of the National Council of Government, presided over by General Namphy, we knew what we were up against. On April 26, a crowd assembled in front of Fort Dimanche to commemorate the massacre perpetrated there twenty-three years earlier by Papa Doc. In 1963, François Duvalier had reacted to an attempt to kidnap his children by executing hundreds of his opponents.

In 1986, the crowd was machine-gunned by the army in front of this sinister building. The shots whistled around my ears. I saw the people running or lying flat. A little later, the city trucks came and loaded up the bodies as if they were picking up garbage. It symbolized the authorities' lack of respect for human life in this country. When the living do not enjoy the most elementary rights, the dead, even those who have died for the freedom of their sisters and brothers, are nothing but debris. Namphy, who talked about holding elections in order to calm international opinion or the financial backers, had blood on his hands. As we had anticipated since February 7, he had chosen his camp and his method: Duvalierism without Duvalier. Only one question remained: had the whole army swung to the side of the Macoutes?

The Macoutes and the army—the popular movement was

about to clash with a third adversary: the Catholic hierarchy, which was little disposed to carry the struggle against the dictator and its authors to a conclusion. Had Bishop Gayot not been crying since February 9: "This is the hour of reconciliation. From now on, the danger we have to watch out for is communism!" When one realizes the liberality with which, in Haiti, the label "communist" is applied, one can guess in which camp the spokesman of the episcopacy had located himself. As usual, he preached resignation in his own style. With the exception of one bishop — or one and a half, as I said at the time — the episcopal conference was divided between Macoutism and immobilism.

At the end of 1985, when all the media were gagged, St. Jean Bosco had emerged as one of the symbols of resistance. Both the chapel and the National School of Arts and Crafts, of which I was the director, were canonically dependent on the parish of St. Joseph. To go from one church to the other took ten minutes on foot, no more. To hear the good news, the word freely spoken, the faithful had gotten into the habit of coming to St. Jean Bosco, turning more and more toward one of the stars that was still shining in the silent darkness.

In the course of these celebrations, each person could hear others say aloud what had to be whispered elsewhere. The people took charge of the word. We were all exposed to the same risks as in other places where resistance was practiced.

Obviously, I devoted little time to administering the sacraments, as would be normal for a parish pastor. If it happened that I did so, in response to a request from someone or other, it could as easily take place at St. Jean Bosco as in some other place.

After the fall of Jean-Claude Duvalier, the word continued to be spoken frankly. The starving themselves spoke of their hunger, often uneasily and without eloquence, but they spoke. And why should we have discussed anything else, when there was a shortage of rice and potatoes? Like Jesus, we spoke of our own reality, and we poured out all the words of Christ in light of our own situation of suffering and injustice. Each person participated in the misfortune of the other; a profoundly biblical expression turned all the faithful against oppression. That word was quite naturally anchored in our human condition. The Creole language supported the feeling of liberation. The subjects had become active and self-expressive; that self-expression took place in their own language. For a priest, proclaiming the word of God is also listening to those without shelter and without work, those who have no voice — to read the word cf God in the reflections of the assembled community.

That fraternity and sorority were clearly distinguished by their charity. No one could any longer satisfy his or her conscience by giving a bit of bread or a few pennies. Even earlier, in 1979, I had refused the soiled and faded clothing the rich offered me to distribute to the poor.

All these new militants, most of them young, workers, peasants, more often unemployed or starving people, moved from consciousness-raising to organization. Newly organized in the *Ti legliz*, "the little ones of the church," they adopted the slogan: "This is only a beginning; let us continue the fight!" For us, there was no question of accepting reconciliation without justice. A new and genuine state could not be built without the *dechoukaj* (uprooting) of all the machinery of a corrupt regime that had embedded itself down to the roots of society.

There was an absolute break between those expert in the theology of liberation and those who hoped for a compromise with the system they served. Would they dare refuse to allow Christians with clean hands the opportunity, the chance to live the gospel as Jesus Christ preached it?

The structures of the church were a perfect reflection of ancient society, the heritage of the fourth century and of the self-seeking and mercantile interests associated with Emperor Constantine. Our church today has accumulated far too much material wealth. The priest has already eaten when he gets up to address an audience that, for its part, does not

know when it may eat again. I reflected on this contradiction
later in a poem:

> What a blessing for the Haitian church,
> Rich, thanks to the poor,
> In a country that is poor because of the rich.

How should we support agrarian reform when the bishops
and religious orders have become the major landowners?
This is a contradiction as unbearable as the maintenance of
the all-powerful institutions of learning that produce the most
reactionary elements in the country and abandon eighty-five
percent of the people to illiteracy.

What a gulf exists between John Paul II's *"fòk sa chanje"*
and the practices of the episcopacy and the nunciature! I do
not know whether the Pope's cry called for a change of
regime, but I quickly understood that the policies of his
ambassador were very similar to those of the United States.
This was conveyed, deliberately or not, by the alliance of the
two imperialisms: political and religious.

The colonial mission system, having disappeared from all
the continents, endures in Haiti. Theology serves to "zom-
bify" the people's spirits in order to subjugate them more
readily to traditional sovereignties. When one says such
things, does it mean that one is rending the unity of the
church and destabilizing it, or on the contrary, does it mean
one is seeking a new path to unity through the conversion of
all to the popular ideals? In 1986 I wrote clearly that one
dare not allow the movement of emancipation to be hobbled
by the very ones who should have been its servants.

We no longer desire to be associated with these hierarchical structures, in which the orders must always
come from above downward to us below; but since our
mission consists in opening the eyes of those at the bottom, the people of God, to listen to what the people
say, to live the people's troubles, to share their anguish

and their hopes, we have little interest in those who are at the helm of church affairs, halfway between the summit and the bottom.

That does not mean that there is only chaos and that each one may do as he or she pleases. Instead, we have a spirit of communion among us, as the people of God, and the closer one is to the top, the more one is a servant. As a result, the president of the episcopal conference cannot go forward alone. He should, whether he wishes to or not, move in rhythm with the Christian collectivity. It is true that in certain circumstances he may have the right to decide. At that moment, if, in his position, he achieves an encounter with those at the bottom, it will be the joy of all. If he does not meet with the bottom, there may well be conflict.

I have certainly been accused of being a bad Catholic (priest) or a demagogic politician, one who praises communism. I respond quite simply that Marxism is not a source of inspiration for me. Instead, the texts of Marx constitute one tool among others to which I may have recourse. To flee from or ignore any philosophy is to prove oneself a cretin.

The accusations that I am a bad Catholic have to do with the company I keep. I have never measured people by their religious affiliation, but solely—if I have the right to judge— by their behavior. By the same token, I do not consider voodoo to be an antagonist or an enemy of the Christian faith. It is a religion or a practice that, as long as Haiti is being examined, merits a certain minimum of explanation.

Orthodox Catholics or well-meaning Westerners consider voodoo to be a complex of superstitions or a catalogue of exotic mysteries. It is regarded as a monadnock or a mountain. *"Déyè mòn gen mòn"* (Beyond the hills there are more hills). Rather than scaling the obstacle to discover what it is hiding, to uncover its origins, they prefer to stop and give judgment. In the veins of voodoo flows a blood that is Christian. The two are complementary in their opposition to evil.

An example? The *hougan* priest will often ask you: "Are you wrong or right?" — applying, in fact, that principle of psychology that explains psychosomatic ills as the result of guilt feelings. Is that so different from the examination of conscience recommended to the Christian?

The Catholic church, protected by the conquistadors or the colonial lords, the altar allied with the throne, fought against voodoo. By what right could it claim such superiority? When St. Paul presented himself at Athens, he tried to understand the culture of the Greeks. No tree can exist without roots. Voodoo, Creole — those are our roots, *rasin lakay* (roots of our homes).

No more than other religions, voodoo cannot substitute for medicine, hygiene, agronomy or climatology. Usurpations and mercenary appropriations are found in voodoo as elsewhere. We should carefully distinguish the voodoo priest from the *bòkòr*, a charlatan who deceives people through sleight-of-hand and whose aim is to get rich. The true *hougan* is a priest, an extraordinarily whole person, who channels, orients, revives, and gives life to the community's faith. By another route, he has acquired certain psychological intuitions: the psychoanalysis he practices, in his own manner, can lead to healing.

I remember a young girl I met in 1978. She wanted me to help her with her psychological problems, and I, modest apprentice that I was, hoped to put into practice some of the theories I had just been studying. Immediately, she burst into tears, and her tears were the expression of the division within her. To provoke a reaction, I tried hypnosis, that sleep in which the superego ceases to exist, and the ego regains its liberty. During her hypnotic sleep, I made a suggestion that became an auto-suggestion for her. Five hours after she awakened, she was to come back to see me with three small stones in her pocket. I awakened her, and she went home. A few hours later, the bell rang. It was she. When I asked her why she had three stones in her pocket, she stared at me blankly. Why were they there? How did I know they were there when she didn't? Psychological practice had allowed me to do what a voodoo priest could do, with no university degree but acting out of a totally different experience. There is no magic in it. When a person believes in you, she or he is ready to take your word as a command.

Another time, in 1982, at the door of a church, again using hypnosis, I was able to restore speech to a child who had been mute for three or four days. She spoke to me in her sleep, and when she was reawakened, she continued speaking. She was pregnant, and her parents had driven the boy away. She regressed. When the trauma was encountered again, her speech was restored. Priest and psychologist: priest, healer and presider—in other lands they might have taken me for a wonder-working king. But there was no risk of that in Haiti! If Freud could have sat down with a voodoo priest, I am sure that they would have debated for hours on the complementarity or parallels in their two approaches!

The Catholic priest, with his Roman formation, steeped in Western bourgeois society, imbued with its prejudices, strengthened by its superiority complex, has never condescended to abandon his pedestal. Conduct a dialogue with a *hougan*, the representative of a society close to nature, black and Haitian? What an idea! In what way could his formation have prepared him to compare his theological convictions with the beliefs of savages from Africa?

What he also refuses to understand is that people who do not possess the vocabulary necessary for expressing what they feel and what they understand take refuge in other formulations, which may or may not be related to invisible or magical dimensions.

It remains to wash voodooism clean of one last sin. It is said to have collaborated with Duvalier, and that Papa Doc made use of it to secure his dictatorship. That may be true. If the accusation comes from the Catholic hierarchy, it could make you laugh—or cry—or keep silent, for charity's sake— Christian charity.

After the massacre at Fort Dimanche, the admonitions and threats began to reach me directly. The army had first gunned down the crowd; now it was shooting false salvos in the psychological war. Together with others, I was denounced as being one of those responsible for the massacre. Namphy wanted some culprits. The massacre was the fault of the victims; the officers who had given the order to clear out the democratic riff-raff were innocent.

The Salesians themselves demanded that I remain silent. The first written warning was sent to me on May 16, 1986. They ordered me not to take part in politics in the future. As if Archbishop Ligondé was not involved in politics! The politics of the corrupt right wing did not excite the least stirrings of conscience, but the politics of the excluded, the voice of the voiceless, when it was heard and repeated, was no longer tolerable.

On the same day a new incident of criminal arson destroyed a slum in the very center of the quarter of La Saline. Apart from guaranteed impunity, this kind of petty gangsterism offered two advantages: it chased the poor people out of the few square yards in which they were living, and it played on international sympathy, attracting funds which inevitably never reached the victims.

A few minutes later, I was on the spot. There were relatives weeping over the ashes of forms that were scarcely human any more. The mother could no longer distinguish her child from the other fragments of charred material. The odor of burnt flesh mingled with the suffocating Haitian heat which was intensified by the fire. How could I help or console the relatives? I was speaking to them when I spied a crew from the national television network. "Certainly, they want to question me, to interview me, to ask my opinion, broadcast my commentary," I said to myself, "but my superiors have just forbidden me to make any political denunciations. All the same, I cannot lower myself to the point of saying that this is just a sad event that is haphazard, ordinary and accidental."

I fled. The tragedy was coupled for me with a drama of conscience, a dilemma the Salesians would resolve much later. Had I not taken a vow of perpetual obedience to the order? I was divided between submission and rage, shame and revolt: why did I flee before God, burnt to ashes by criminal arsonists?

The doubt, anguish and remorse pierced my conscience. Some young people who understood my confusion went in person to the television station to spread the news: "Father Aristide has been forbidden to speak; they want to exile him. . . . We are going on strike to demand the lifting of the sanctions." I had not given them any orders. They occupied my house, forbidding me even to go outside for fear the Salesians would ship me out on the first plane. For the first time, a breach was opened between the congregation and the community. My superior was muzzling a voice that the community had liberated. After all, were we not there, in the image of St. Jean Bosco, for the service of the poor? following the direct line of the gospel?

In face of the young people's determination, the Salesians gave in. But the scar had not been cauterized, and the sequel would certainly not be a happy one, considering that the CNG (National Council of Government) was now made up only of tricksters. Namphy did not want elections. There were two hundred thousand of us who protested in November against this arbitrary government.

Another event occurred in 1986 that was utterly extraordinary in Haiti. Thirty thousand women took to the street to demand equal wages, equal responsibilities, and equal opportunity. Up to that time, I had lived in a men's world run by men, centered on Christian communities in which they monopolized the essential responsibilities. A movement like this one challenged me, raised questions, and disturbed me.

As a child, I had sometimes met Anne-Marie's friends and observed the injustice done to daughters and mothers, even though they were responsible for all provisions, that is, for the essentials of life. Often it was the women alone who maintained the continuity of the family and provided for the education of the children. When seventy-five percent of children never go to school, and when the Haitian family is so often headed by a single parent, who provides the minimum of education and subsistence? The mother. The men legislate or command, while the women suffer. The unequal spheres of freedom reflect a *macho* society. Equality of opportunity in a society where women work so hard thus appeared to me to be a claim as essential as it was novel.

It remains to allot to women a place within the democracy, to give them the dignity they deserve. The presence of four women in the Préval government in 1991 would be more than a symbolic response. It would be accompanied by promotion of many others to political and economic responsibilities.

This society knows nothing but despotism and its victims: victims of bullets, torture, hunger, arson. In Port-au-Prince there are victims who are even more victimized than those: children without homes or relatives. There are thousands of them in the capital, without the least refuge. Next to them, the *restavek* are privileged. There is always something worse than the worst. In Brazil, I know, the death squads shoot at children the way stray dogs are shot in other places. In the Haitian capital, we had not yet attained that point of degradation.

I often saw these children on the main street of Port-au-Prince, not far from our house at St. Jean Bosco. Their presence had challenged me for a long time: how could we speak of God and leave God wandering in the streets? It was all the more poignant because these were children, innocents subjected to every kind of corruption just to survive. What could we do *with* these children? —with them, and not for them.

We had discussed it for a long time with the young people who belonged to various organizations. They had their own point of view: poor as we are, what do we have to share with those who are still poorer? Dialogue and affection, to begin with. It is not easy. These "wild children" could scarcely be approached, for they were pathologically defiant toward anyone who might want to seduce or recruit them. The difficulties of a short life like that of a hunted beast released in them reflexes of fear and/or rejection. They scented a trap. They hesitated: why did anyone want to do them good? Where were they being channeled?

"The Family Selavi" was born on July 20, 1986, a Sunday. Earlier, we had organized recreational activities to which friends brought a little food or a little money. As at every Sunday service, I was host to some priests: generally, these were men who shared our reading of the gospel. Traditionally, the community gave a gift to the celebrants. As things would have it, one of those invited was Father William Smarth, a great figure in the popular church and a veteran of struggle against the dictatorship. I had chosen a street child to present him with the modest present, a boy of about nine named Selavi (*"C'est la vie"* — "that's life"). Yes, that was his name.

I asked him some questions:

How old are you?
I don't know.
Who is your mother?
I don't know.
What do you do on the streets?
Sometimes I wash cars.
How do you eat?
When I get work, I eat.
And if not?
I don't eat.
Where do you sleep?
Sometimes I am so hungry that I can't sleep.

A woman in the church began to cry. Then some young people burst into tears. A few minutes later, a ripple ran through the congregation. Spontaneously, the faithful came to little Selavi to give him money and offer assistance. In face of the collective emotion, I began to speak: "Let us stop being consumers of the host and become producers of love. Let us arrange a meeting, a meeting *nouselavi.* And together, we will see what we can do."

That is how *Lafanmi Selavi* began. I started welcoming children into the community, and from that time the situation became widely known: international organizations came to our aid — Caritas, France-Libertés with Danièle Mitterrand, a woman whose greatness and devotion I admire. A raising of the community's consciousness, and then that of the nation, led to a worldwide solidarity.

I had the feeling that I was acting as a theologian in order to give direction to a political struggle: the eruption of the poor onto the social scene. We had been able to buy a house in a good neighborhood. The bourgeois or middle class, who only occasionally glimpse the poor neighborhoods, saw the dispossessed people from the slums of La Saline arriving in their own area. Certainly, they were astonished and apprehensive, but the two social groups met very quickly. *Lafanmi Selavi* became an extraordinary crossroads for initiatives and for friendship, one of the memories that moves me the most when I rummage through my past.

The middle-class families, including fourteen doctors, gave themselves unstintingly. I brought there, by car, the poorest of the poor, people I found at the church doors. *Lafanmi Selavi* was an experience and a symbol of realized Christian faith genuinely shared. The new frontiers we were discovering together rendered the anachronistic repression engulfing the country all the more odious. We proved to the skeptics that it was possible to live differently in our society. On Camille Léon Street, *Lafanmi Selavi* offered hundreds of children the possibility of recovering a decent life. A life, and then, the chance to go to school and learn a trade. Afterwards other centers began to open.

I remember a significant anecdote from a time several

months later. After my car, a little Charade, had been destroyed by an assassination attempt, I was given a big, rich person's car, an Isuzu Trooper. The vehicle was crammed with ragged children; there were seventeen or nineteen of us inside. In front of the presidential palace, another Isuzu resembling mine overtook me and forced me to stop. Was it a Macoute, a friend of the generals, a new assassination attempt? I imagined the worst. But the driver, smiling, called to me: "Thanks for the show, and bravo! That is the first time in this country that I have seen such a vehicle used so well."

One should not suppose that I never think of anything but Port-au-Prince. Of course, that is where I live. That is where I was first active. But the journey to and return from Les Cayes in 1985, several visits to the hill country, including my own village, and meetings with rural priests or organizers maintained my relationship with the country. I have often expressed my solidarity with the rice growers of Artibonite, those peasants who were being crushed by the imperialistic dumping of surplus products provided under the pretext of humanitarian aid. Humanitarian aid can be the best or the worst of things. When it floods the market with the overproduction of others at low prices, it deprives the local producers of their natural clientele. There is such a thing as a freedom that isolates and starves others. The *manje sinistre*, food aid furnished in times of disaster, drives the peasants to their knees. The same thing had been done previously to the pig farmers.

In that case, the Americans claimed that an outbreak of swine fever required the slaughtering of all the pigs in Haiti. This was not true, but those animals played a major role in the rural economy. An alimentary equilibrium that was already precarious was thereby destroyed, and a peasantry was assassinated without appeal, both in the real and in the figurative sense. Demonstrations were, as usual, severely punished: the peasants were massacred.

The elimination of the pigs amounted, as we say, to burning the savings book. Its purpose was to draw into the cities the abundant and cheap labor force necessary for the assembly plants. But the peasants began to organize themselves; associations and labor unions—*Tèt ansanm* ("heads together")—burst forth in revolt, as did organizations of young people in the city—*solidarite ant jèn* (solidarity among the young).

Namphy, Régala (his principal deputy), and the CNG, who had never managed to organize the elections they did not want, had no resources with which to face the growth of popular initiatives except the weapon of the mafia and dictatorship: assassination, individual or collective.

CHAPTER 7

"Take Left"

The summer of 1987 was torrid. I hoped, without investing too much faith in it, that the brutality would lessen in the wake of the repeated massacres, but instead we were moving toward a paroxysm of violence.

Still, there was a bright period in May, marked by the creation of a provisory electoral council made up of representatives of democratic organizations. It had scarcely been installed when the CNG curtailed its privileges and renewed the repression of the militant opposition. One of the major trade unions, CATH (Autonomous Confederation of Haitian Workers), was dissolved.

On June 30, Bishop Romélus called for the resignation of the CNG. His colleague Gayot took to the airwaves to support Namphy and his accomplices. More than ever before, there appeared to be some resistance, even within the inner circle of the episcopal conference — not to mention the case of Bishop Ligondé, to whom the synod of Port-au-Prince had just recommended that he take a sabbatical leave abroad so that his Macoute connections might be forgotten. However, he had refused. Bishop Romélus supported Operation *Rache Manyòk*: rooting out the manioc to recover the virgin land, i.e., extirpating corruption in order to build democracy.

A general strike broke out. When the shopkeepers, taxis, *tap-taps*, and street vendors quit, about twenty people died.

Stores were closed, streets deserted, tires burned in the arteries near the center of the city. The CNG bent but did not break: the provisional electoral council (CEP) was confirmed, and CATH was reauthorized. The politicians hesitated to push their power to the limit. Was it not true that Marc Bazin, the American's man, was calling for a return to work? So was the episcopal conference, which saw us menaced by "the specter of anarchy and of civil war, the cost of which will be borne by "the little people. . . . No institution possesses any miraculous remedy."

The United States, like the Catholic hierarchy, continued to place its confidence in Namphy, flanked by a CEP which he short-circuited at the first opportunity. The wave of assassinations that followed did not disprove my premonitions. Again, fear was everywhere.

Reagan considered me a communist. The CNG demanded that I be banished, the Macoutes that I be eliminated. As for the Catholic hierarchy, they marched in step. Once again the Salesians intervened, thus placing me in an untenable situation, just as I had been a year before.

In August 1987, a superior came, this time directly from Rome. I defended myself, trying to make him understand that I, as a Haitian, was in a better situation to understand the state of things in my own country. I accomplished nothing. The Vatican had just condemned liberation theology. Father Varesco gave me three days to prepare for my transfer to Croix-des-Missions, about twelve kilometers from Port-au-Prince.

Should I accede, in the hope of returning soon? Was there a duty of disobedience that was stronger than the vows I had taken? Would my friends accuse me of not assisting the people when they were in danger? I thought there might be another strategy: to obey the authorities, while remaining in communion with the popular will. I feared that my superiors might use a lack of submission on my part to discredit me. I had asked in vain for time to bring the young people to accept my departure. My suitcase closed, I met with a little group: "I am going north to preach at Ste. Suzanne. We will meet when I come back, at Croix-des-Missions. Then I will be going to Rome, via Canada. Don't provoke any agitation. Try, when I am gone, to help our friends to digest this news."

They did not accept it themselves; how were they to explain it to others? The news of my transfer spread along the street. I learned of the reaction on my return, while I was still in the car, accompanied by a religious sister from Quebec, Aline Tramblay. Radio Soleil was reporting a hunger strike in the cathedral and a certain amount of unrest.

I returned to Croix-des-Missions. My baggage was waiting for me. But the young people were occupying the cathedral. Once again, the Salesians had to give in. But Gérard Noël, the minister of information, had made one last bid to discredit me. I was supposed to have said, while preaching the arming of the poor: "Everyone should have a firearm so as to participate in the armed struggle . . . in a total revolution." He accused me, to be sure, of advocating "hatred and violence and inciting to revolt." He was lying. I have never encouraged armed struggle. My recorded sermons prove it. This was pure "disinformation"!

For six days, the cathedral was never empty. The people came and went, relieving one another. It was an anthill in which the new arrivals had to work hard to find a place. The atmosphere was at the same time serious and good-humored. My friends' stories and the television pictures were my sole tie to the occupants. There was no possibility for me to enter the cathedral during that strike, which I had not instigated. To ask the young people to stop their movement would have been a gift to my enemies, indicating to them that if I had the power to stop a strike, I could also have the power to launch a strike.

I knew them well, these young people, this *Ti legliz* (little church). They were mature and capable of assuming their own responsibilities. They had not obeyed me. They were not simply defending Aristide, but a greater, more global reality, even if I had become a symbol in their eyes. They also demanded more than my return to St. Jean Bosco. They insisted that the bishops should make a statement about the murders of the summer. Why had the massacre of two hundred peasants at Jean-Rabel been swathed in silence? If muteness did not mean complicity, the moment had come for the episcopacy to prove it, and thus to prevent new dramas — or at least to contribute to preventing them.

Rome gave in. The bishops went a little way by saying a few timid words about the peasants of Jean-Rabel, and I could, after all, enter the cathedral — not like a prince of the church, certainly not. As the symbol of a tight-knit community? Undoubtedly that. On that evening, the building exploded in a real delirium of joy, even though just a few minutes earlier they had seized a man with a pistol in his hand who intended to shoot me. The army was not slow to arrive to recover the weapon, after having surrounded the cathedral! The joy could only be shared, no matter how much violence was on the prowl.

But the hunger strike marked a turning point. The movement showed that I represented not only a danger, but a power that would not be content with a patched-up Duvalierism or a democracy subservient to orders coming from the outside. Did the bishops realize that we were incontestably the majority in the churches? They were being offered a chance to say something on behalf of democracy. It was up to them to seize it.

The next Sunday began with a great Christian celebration of reunion with the community. There were thousands of us. In the afternoon, at the invitation of some of my priest friends, I left Port-au-Prince to go to Pont-Sondé for a gathering in memory of the peasant martyrs of Jean-Rabel. It took an hour and a half to get there, but I would be among friends, and there were a great many people hoping to meet me.

The assembly was held under a huge shed open to the four winds. A relay of trucks brought families coming from the surrounding region. The children were splashing in the canal. Jean-Marie Vincent, one of the organizers of the *Tèt ansanm* ("heads together") movement, was there. This great Montfort priest, symbol of the struggle against feudal power, recalled vividly how, a month earlier, two hundred peasants had died, the victims of a genuine hunt for human beings through the hills around Jean-Rabel; he told how the great landlords had organized the massacre, and why the assassins had not been pursued.

There were posters welcoming me. The audience applauded the little skits in which united peasants and workers went head to head with the oligarchy. I felt more relaxed. We sat chatting together.

The celebration began. There was a French television crew there who were following me for the day. I had kept to one side to allow them to set up. And then the journalists and cameramen left. It was my turn to speak. The priest had scarcely introduced me when the Macoutes moved in, their guns turned on the podium. There was a series of explosions. I felt nothing, but I had a very clear view of their hats, the white shirts and the weapons spitting fire. Flee, throw oneself down—in such situations, a thousand and one thoughts cross one's mind. Death is imminent. I remain standing, my arms crossed. My eyes meet those of one of the armed men who is still there, one of those perhaps who was to have shot me. Was there, in the meeting of our glances, an energy leaping from one to the other? The killer hesitated, appeared to waver, and lowered his gun. In a kind of televised slow motion, he walked clumsily backward, as if he were paralyzed. *Mwen gen pwen pran bal*? (Am I invincible, insensible to bullets?) One might have thought so. Some people were running; others had fallen. One good woman, lying on the ground, grabbed my feet so that I would fall down like the others and avoid the projectiles. Nothing remained for me, as I lay alongside two French people and their children, but to try to catch sight of the fleeing bandits one last time. By some miracle, no one was dead, and only a few wounded.

Night fell. We decided to return to Port-au-Prince. A little convoy of five cars left Port-Sondé very fast. Antoine Adrien and William Smarth (two old Holy Ghost priests who had returned from exile to serve their people), Jean-Marie Vincent and a young English-speaking Canadian, Brother Burg, were with me.

At the edge of the town of Saint-Marc there was a barrier where the police were checking vehicles. In a pouring rain, the officers were noting the numbers on the license plates and searching in vain for guns. We had to get out in the pitch dark. We could scarcely distinguish the shapes going away on foot in the direction of Port-au-Prince. What was going to happen? Were there snipers in ambush? Nothing. After searching our car, they let us go.

But a hundred yards farther on, as we came around a curve, we found trees and oil drums laid across the road, obliging the vehicles to stop again. This was the real roadblock. We very quickly saw several dozen men armed with machetes, rocks, spears, rifles, revolvers, all gleaming in the headlights. We understood right away that they were waiting for us: the people at the first barrier had let them know who we were.

Things happened much faster than I can tell them. The faces were running with water and the rain was gluing their clothes to their bodies; some of them wore nothing but shorts, others had army uniforms. In the blink of an eye, they fell on us. The windows exploded. They showed a preference for our vehicle: it was subjected to a hail of stones and the headlights were snuffed out by the blows of the machetes.

I was sitting in the back, in the middle. They made William Smarth, seated next to me on the left, get out of the car. A man seized him by the collar, machete in hand. Would his head become one more stone to be thrown with the others? In any case, it appeared to me that his life was hanging by a thread. But no. The Macoutes pushed him brutally back into his seat.

On the other side, Father Adrien was dragged out of our

4x4 and beaten. Up front, Jean-Marie Vincent and Brother Burg were struck by stones; their faces were bleeding. I bent down to avoid the rain of projectiles, and the rear window collapsed over me. The machete that broke it would have struck me if I had not tried, two seconds earlier, to fit myself onto the floor of the car. Maybe they thought they had killed me. In the cacophony of missiles and shouts, I heard only one word: communist.

They went looking for gasoline and matches to finish us off, and lost a few seconds in the process. The better to burn us in our mobile coffin, they had thrown Adrien back into the car. Jean-Marie Vincent, whose coolness is extraordinary, was certainly one of their primary targets. He had noticed a narrow passage on the left that allowed cars coming from Port-au-Prince to pass the barricade.

We saw people being beaten unmercifully by the Macoutes.

"Take left, take left!" shouted Jean-Marie to our driver, an English-speaking Canadian recently arrived in Haiti and justifiably dazed by the situation.

Without headlights, blinded by the downpour from the skies and from the Macoutes, the 4x4 dashed forward, bucked over the stones, staggered over the branches and roared on, all its windows broken, all the faces inside running with blood, splitting the crowd.

The four-wheel drive saved us. Curious spectators who had run to the scene told us later that they had recognized the Macoutes in charge of the sector and the soldiers from the local garrison. To turn the people away, they had assured them that it was nothing but a settling of accounts between groups of hooligans. In the end, the Macoutes believed that I was invincible and invisible. As the Creole proverb says, "*pi piti pi rèd*" ("the smallest one is the most fearless").

But why deny it? We were very much afraid. Still, those attacking us, with only one or two exceptions, were only poor, manipulated wretches, proletarians corrupted by effective brainwashing and a few dollars. Bandits trained for pre-programmed crimes, understanding nothing of the serious offenses they were ordered to commit, they were not the really guilty ones. The conductors of the orchestra live and govern in peace. Nothing remained of our car except a body and a motor driving blindly in the darkness. Should we continue this way, or go on foot in search of a refuge? An hour later, the good Samaritan appeared: a house where some Protestant missionaries were living. We were welcomed, even though our hosts feared reprisals. They sent word to the pastor at Montrouis and, a few hours later, took us to his house.

From there the news spread throughout the country, and many of our friends came to meet us. My wounds were only superficial, but, as it turned out, I needed several hours to recover my spirits. The minister of information attempted to credit the incident to a demonstration by opponents of liberation theology, interspersed with some minor incidents. No one believed it.

The news rocked the country, especially the young people in the cities, the slum-dwellers, and the country people I had met the day before at Pont-Sondé, but it did not surprise anyone. The electoral deadlines and the growing dependence of the country on the good opinion of Uncle Sam were making the military in the CNG nervous. What the church had not been able to achieve by exiling me, the Macoutes hoped to resolve by more expeditious means. It was all the more tempting since three of my companions belonged to the best-known and most detested group of all—the theologians of liberation.

The security measures taken in Port-au-Prince to prevent any kind of demonstration, even before the assassination attempt had been reported on the radio, proved (had there been any need for proof) that this was all part of a conspiracy, and that in circles close to the palace it was thought that Adrien, Smarth, Vincent and Aristide were already dead. No doubt, Namphy and Régala would have deplored the assassination, just as they "regretted the incident"!

Just a few days earlier, on returning to my church, I had spoken in a sermon about my own death. It is true that it appeared a probable event to many people, both friends and enemies. And it had come very close, twice in one day.

Speaking of my own death, and then death met face to face, enabled me to commune in the most visceral way with all the victims of macoutism. I have sometimes been accused of trying to become a martyr. I love life. I do not want to die, except to help those who are struggling with me. The assassination attempts accelerated the process of consciousness-raising, but I did not go looking for them. On the other hand, I am prepared to take measures to protect myself, so long as they do not silence my voice. I have never had any intention of keeping silent.

But death is a present potential. When I examine the paths of liberation, I know that it must be faced. Those who have laid hold of the country will not give it back to us as a gift. Death, my death, might happen along the way. Who knows? How can I not think of it?

I do not consider myself indispensable; no one is. But, without any false humility, I believe that I can render some service on the side of the people on the march. If some people, in the end, take Aristide for a symbol, they are wrong and right at the same time. The unity of a people on behalf of justice is a power that cannot be conquered forever. Human beings, on the other hand, are mortal.

I have often said that the people should not rely on miracles; there is no magic wand or wonder-worker who can create plenty. The only miracle is the raising of the people's consciousness of their own power, and the taking of their destiny into their own hands. We have to take what the privileged few want to keep for themselves alone.

The strategy of the CNG was part of a terrorist logic: the methodical elimination of the leaders of the opposition. These included Bernard Sansaricq (failed assassination attempt), Louis Athis, Yves Volel. ... The military did not hesitate to draw the conclusion—which agreed with their hypothesis—that, certainly, the Haitian people were not mature enough to hold elections.

Even so, *pèp la te swaf eleksyon an* (the people were thirsty for elections). Planned for November 29, 1987, they were won by the Macoutes. In the morning, the voters at Argentine-Bellegarde school were massacred by hooded men: twenty-four dead. The killing took place after a night punctuated by shots and explosions. The sinister Régala had promised to "respect good order." The army let it all go on. The elections were cancelled. The collusion was so obvious, the offense so manifest, that even President Reagan could not accept it.

Uncle Sam wanted elections that looked like elections—like Canada Dry: the smell, the taste, but not the reality. Namphy did better—or worse—than Reagan demanded. If the Americans could not tolerate the offense, it was because they wanted a responsible democracy led by people whom they could control, but disencumbered of the mafia scum.

The publication of the electoral law, on December 18, 1987, entailed a lengthy discourse on the historic compromise or minimum consensus of which Namphy spoke. The vote attained, effectively, an historic minimum: there were neither voter lists nor containers for the ballots. And, as if the swindler were afraid that everyone would object to the swindle, every incitement to abstain from voting, every appeal for a boycott was to be punishable with imprisonment! The general, expert at elections, really surpassed the bounds of imagination: we were to move from the tragedy of November to the farce of February.

Everything remained on Namphy's books: there would be no independent electoral commission. The principal favorites of November retired from the lists. The army went around arresting the militant members of the popular organizations, and the representatives of power were invited to take the voters to the polls by force. Fear was universal, but it was not sufficient to force the Haitians to the ballot boxes. Will the exact percentage of voters ever be known? It was between five and ten percent. The victory was total, but it was a negative victory.

The military declared Manigat elected. Four months later, this man, elected by one Haitian out of twenty, dismissed Namphy. He removed Namphy, but despite his intrigues in the palace and the barracks, Manigat did not last three days. Namphy knew the places and connections of power too well; on June 20 he resumed complete control. The government no longer contained anything but military men.

CHAPTER 8

The Calvary of St. Jean Bosco

There is seldom one without the other: as a symbol of resistance, St. Jean Bosco also became a target of attack. Brutal treatment was meted out to the parishioners, cars were destroyed, individuals placed under suspicion, more and more stones thrown at the modest church, not counting the increasingly frequent efforts at intimidation. There were threats, more threats, constant threats.

Up to this time, we had avoided the worst, even on September 4, 1988, when my friends disarmed an unknown man carrying a pistol. I was at the center of the nave when a group of young people came toward me. One of them was brandishing the gun in my direction, and for a moment I thought that he wanted to kill me. What was I thinking? It was a terrible mistake: he did not realize what emotions he had aroused, for he was simply returning the weapon that I had put down on the altar.

Should we continue the eucharistic celebration? What should we do with the man? In fact, we had scarcely any choice. To hold him would be to provoke an intervention by the powers of enforcement: always elsewhere when the Macoutes perpetrated their assassination attempts undisturbed, now they would not fail to intervene promptly.

Sequestering individuals, seizing weapons: from being victims, we would very quickly have become the guilty. The powers would have accused us, for example, of establishing an
arsenal for armed struggle, or a training school for urban
guerilla warfare. The assassin risked nothing! In spite of the
danger, we would continue our Sunday celebration. The
assembly dispersed, and everyone left the church unhindered.

Tuesday was the day for the young people's Mass. Every
Tuesday evening, a rain of stones fell on St. Jean Bosco. The
intimidation had become regular, even punctual. Should we
continue, now that the Macoutes had passed through a new
stage of escalation? Frankly, I was hesitant. How far may the
pastor expose his own flock to danger, even if persistence is
part of our nonviolent response? I was inclined to seek a
tactical response, to give in and renew our assemblies a week
or two later. "It is too dangerous; the Macoutes are determined to strike harder. It is better not to hold the celebration."

This was language that the young people may have understood, but did not accept. I quickly sensed that they rejected
what appeared to them to be a surrender. If a Christian community has definitely decided to celebrate its faith, even in
the midst of danger, how can one take flight and abandon
young people who are so determined? I could only follow
them.

So I agreed to celebrate the Mass, but not to preach; it
was a question of showing that we existed, that we would not
concede to any pressure, but that we would furnish no basis
for any accusation that we were behaving provocatively. The
Mass was short, scarcely a half hour long. It had just ended
when a hail of stones struck the building and those who were
leaving. On that evening we were stoned, just like the first
Christian communities of antiquity.

It was not necessary to be a great scholar to gauge the
situation: we were experiencing a crescendo of attacks. On
Saturday, September 10, there was a meeting of the church
officers to deal with a single question: should there be a Mass

the next day, Sunday the 11th? We thought of having Mass at six A.M. If there was a crowd, we could hold another, as usual, at nine. If not, we would close the doors.

At six o'clock only a sparse crowd was present. It seemed better, therefore, to let this Sunday go by without a big celebration. Everyone seemed to agree. Two hours later, the situation had changed. Some young people called me on the intercom:

"You have to come down. It is a quarter to nine and a lot of people are arriving. They want to have a celebration, just like every other Sunday, at all costs."

"But that is not what we planned yesterday, or even this morning!"

"The people won't hear of it. For them, it is Sunday, and they want to pray; they don't want to go home without receiving communion. Even if the Macoutes intervene, they want to have their celebration."

The most radical elements of the *Ti legliz* had neither pushed nor encouraged the people to come. There was no pressure or manipulation. The people of the neighborhood and a few others came spontaneously, courageously. The majority knew what they were risking. A heroic, evangelical determination called them, drew them, even excited them. This band of the most faithful among the faithful surpassed the thousand mark—even more; there may have been two thousand.

Now and then their faces were serious. They spoke little, but their eyes said: "If we leave you alone, the bandits will kill you. We want to be with you at the foot of the cross." They laid claim to the eucharistic celebration—for themselves and for me.

I had asked the young people to try to identify the people so as to be sure that no provocateurs or conspirators had infiltrated the crowd. They felt certain that none had and the events confirmed it: all those who entered were ours, were very surely our own. And so, I agreed to yield to the community.

When I opened the church, I was conscious of the stakes and of the serious risks in this drama. For weeks, the Macoutes had been escalating their warnings and the blows of their fists or their stones. They felt themselves being defied, and they would take vengeance. I sensed that I was someone who was climbing toward "Calvary." Two of the stronger young people went with me from my room to the sacristy. As we crossed the interior court, it was truly the word Calvary, both as the scene of Christ's passion and as a sorrowful personal ordeal, that constantly returned to my mind. I was obsessed with a presentiment that I was living through my last hours.

I remember perfectly the moment of my arrival, facing the sea of faithful young people or whole families: "If you are here this morning, it means that you have accepted, you have desired to take the cross of Christ on your shoulders. That is what the Gospel of today tells us. Instead of asking God's forgiveness, we can now open our hearts to receive God's good news."

I announced the gospel. I hoped our reflections, our conversation would be shorter than usual, since everyone knew the risks that the people assembled here were running. We were approaching the consecration when the rain of stones began to fall. The stones were not alone; another concert was substituted for our music: the first hail of bullets passed by me on the right, striking the tabernacle and the first victims, who collapsed to the floor.

Should I encourage the people to remain? Should I urge them to leave? How should I know what ought to be done? Some were already shouting that we should remain united, amid the uproar of bodies and benches. I was still holding the microphone in my hand, while a little group of young people was trying to drag me to the altar to avoid the shots that were particularly heavy in that direction. We tried to sing. I could not make up my mind to abandon the community. After all, they had come to me, and I ought to stay with them.

I remembered April 26, 1986, in front of Fort Dimanche, when I was holding the Radio-Soleil microphone in my hand at the moment when the military were massacring the people gathered there. The same experience was being repeated amid the crackling bursts of firing. Fearless, even rash, the young people pulled me away by force, tearing the microphone from me and leading me toward my house. Meanwhile, resistance had been organized inside the church, the doors barricaded, the wounded were being cared for, and the people were ready to seize the attackers if they tried to enter.

A pregnant woman had been hit by direct fire and almost eviscerated. Blood spurting, she tried to escape. Father Julio, a good Salesian, a heroic priest, was busy in the fullest sense of the word, looking for a stretcher. Inside, the active nonviolence for the moment discouraged the bandits from finishing their massacre.

The Mass had not lasted twenty minutes. Around eleven o'clock, the besieged were still occupying the church, defending themselves without weapons, but using stones against those who tried to enter. One young person even succeeded, by what miracle I do not know, in getting several dozen helmets to improve our protection. The church became a battlefield, but we could not leave it, under penalty of dying outside, all of us massacred.

There were about a hundred Macoutes, mostly young people, wearing red or black t-shirts or armbands. They were freer in their activities than they had been since the fall of Jean-Claude Duvalier. The scene would have been dramatically ordinary if it had not been seen or observed by so many passive witnesses. At a distance of a few dozen yards, the men of the church, headed by the apostolic nuncio, viewed the scene from afar. There is no way of dividing the truth, and I am reporting it in its entirety: in fact, on that day, the Pope's ambassador, Paolo Romeo, knew everything and saw everything. Neither he nor the archbishop of Port-au-Prince intervened to stop the massacre.

The provincial delegate of the Salesians, a good man and a courageous priest, even if he often bows to the orders of his superiors, came to give us his support in face of the thugs, manipulated on this day by Namphy. The others did not budge. They waited — hoping for my death? or for the example of a new slaughter that would discourage any argument?

By three o'clock in the afternoon, confusion reigned everywhere, and the church had been half burned. The military had demanded that I come out; if I did not, they would set fire to the house. Should I perish in the fire? or die standing up? I was about to go out when a friendly wink from someone opposite made me realize that I should not cross the threshold. This time a justice of the peace was with the military: "We are entering at this time, with your permission, to search the house and verify that you have no weapons. . . . "

They searched my room. An apparent calm hid my nervousness. This had been going on for hours and I had only partial news of the community, which by now had dispersed. How many were dead? The soldiers were all around me with their weapons. Was one of them going to kill me? Had he received his orders to do it? They seemed to hesitate, unsure of their mission. I wondered if the most determined of them did not fear to bear the responsibility for their crime the next day.

They split up. One group went out, waiting for me at the foot of the stairs; the others did not appear hostile. We had even spoken with one another, in general terms. My books and my knowledge of psychology and anthropology piqued their curiosity. It was a real conversation, almost calm, two steps from a deserted and partly burned church. A witness would tell me later that a veritable stream of blood was flowing out of St. Jean Bosco. Father Jacques Mésidor and others also tried to soften the soldiers, offering them refreshments, talking to them. Finally, at the end of the afternoon, they departed.

Departed! That was also what remained for me to do. I had to walk through the midst of the soldiers, cross one interior courtyard separating the house from the school, then cross a second courtyard to reach the wall that adjoined the main street. The soldiers were there, with faces either hostile or hard as marble, but they did not actually make the murderous move that everyone dreaded. Three people, including a religious sister whose courage I greatly respect, waited for me in a car that left St. Jean Bosco very fast.

Of course the same question arose as at Pont-Sondé. Why, if they had believed that I had died in the first assault on the church in the morning, had they hesitated to shoot at me later? At a few yards' distance, it would have been child's play. Those who had been paid and those who had allowed the morning's massacre to take place (thirteen dead and sixty wounded), many of them drug addicts, the people who had burned the church—what irrational force had stopped those red armbands, some of whom were still hanging around, in the shadow of the soldiers? remorse? division among them? the shock of seeing someone resurrected or miraculously saved? the fear of being branded assassins by the official or clandestine media? reluctance to kill before so many witnesses? fear of *dechoukaj* or of popular revenge? The answer is all these things, as well as the fact that the whole event was happening live.

It was true: the whole country knew about it. The radio had not stopped broadcasting the news, interrupting the program schedule. The Haitians knew that there were many victims, but did not know whether I was still alive. Through their solidarity, the media may have avoided a massacre of still greater proportions. The church was brushwood, easily destroyed. Namphy and his accomplices, unaware that they were enjoying their last days of power, feared a reaction of popular rage, a riot in the central city or a series of *dechoukaj*. Another outcome of this drama could have been a night of violence.

We learned later that the attack had been ordered by Franck Romain, the mayor of Port-au-Prince, one of the barons of Duvalierism. The tense climate and the collapse of the state authority would permit him, so he hoped, to remove Namphy. Moreover, some witnesses recognized municipal employees among the killers.

The executioners were furious at the media and promised new penalties. Two days later, the church at Cité-Soleil, which was served by my fellow Salesian, Arthur Volel, burned in the middle of the night. Franck Romain, having been denounced, immediately denied having anything to do with it, but his denial took the form of a threat: "Whoever sows the wind reaps the whirlwind."

Our car rolled at full speed toward Pétionville. The poor driver, incidentally, would be the victim of an assassin the following year. It was in the residential section that evening that I met the nuncio, magnificent in his cassock, wearing a compassionate smile and assuring me of his full sympathy. Bishop Lafontant was with him. At first, I swear, I hesitated to receive his embrace. Finally, I thought that in the most tragic moments one ought to respond with love, even if I thought him an accomplice. I received Paolo Romeo, all the while repeating in my heart of hearts: "Lord, give us the power to love him without accepting what he has done—or what he has failed to do."

Neither he nor the bishops had the courage to cry out when the wolves were devouring the sheep before their eyes. The opposite of courage is called cowardice.

My death would undoubtedly have fixed things very nicely: the dispute with the Salesians, for example. Not that they had wanted me to disappear in that way: the directors in Rome, under pressure from the Haitian authorities, wanted to keep me alive—but somewhere other than in Haiti, or even in Latin America.

The order had only retreated temporarily after the occupation of the cathedral a year earlier. The popular pressure had been too strong, but the Salesians still dreamt of finding a means to exile me. "Whoever sows the wind reaps the whirlwind," as Franck Romain, that low politician and apprentice dictator, had said. The cause of these offenses, the one responsible for the whirlwind, it turned out, was I! If this reasoning did not shock me but flattered me, coming from a Macoute leader, it seemed incredible to me on the lips of a Salesian superior.

He came from the Dominican Republic and arrived in Port-au-Prince the very day after that bloody Sunday. "Listen," he told me straight away, "we have asked you often enough these past three years not to get mixed up in politics, and to stick to your mission as a priest. Now you see the result: our church burned, our house ransacked. Have you considered how much physical damage you have brought on our community?"

Thirteen people had died in the fire or from gunshots, and that was his first thought! However much love I have for my neighbor, I received this language, coming from a Christian whose mission was to be more Christian than others, as a slap in the face. For want of love, I managed to keep my composure. The issue of the discussion seemed like a replay. There were the same proposals as the previous year: that I should leave Haiti for Rome, and then for Canada, or else for Canada first, and then for Italy; in short, the same refrain.

The private interview ended, and in the presence of my Salesian brothers, I asked for a few hours to reflect before giving my answer. It seemed to me more difficult to give in than it had been a year ago. Once I had left, the enemies of the community would surely proceed to make it pay dearly for the spirit of resistance within it. But worse, they would say: "Look, you others, some are dead, others are wounded or in flight, you are suffering, you are persecuted—and the man who got you so worked up is taking it easy outside the country. He has abandoned you!" The Macoutes, by the way, had made a public announcement that they would bring down Aristide at the first opportunity.

Franck Romain was at work in the shadows. While Namphy thought that he was acting on his behalf, Romain, the mayor of Port-au-Prince, was working on his own account:

channeling the general discontent in order to seize power. At the same time, the young people were opposed to my departure. And then, suddenly, on September 17, 1988, there was a dramatic turn of events: a coup d'état.

Before this, the Salesians had been putting so much pressure on me to leave that I had written out a short statement: I am ready to leave, but what will become of the community at St. Jean Bosco? Have you calculated all the consequences? I was waiting for the response. They desired my departure so strongly that I had no illusions.

With the coup d'état, the course changed 180 degrees. They asked me to remain, even explaining over the radio that there had never been any question of exiling me!

They used me! I was an embarrassment: get out! You can protect us from a new situation: stay here! Quite aware of popular reaction, the bishops, having calculated very well, preferred that I should remain. In their fear of *dechoukaj*, they now felt less confidence in the lower ranks of the army, who had revolted, than in the insignia of the superior officers.

On the part of the Salesians, the intervention of Father Jacques Mésidor, who had been there since the burning of St. Jean Bosco, was the determining factor in Rome's about-face. He had courageously, but in vain, opposed my exile.

After a period of hesitation, everyone recognized that Avril, who had replaced Namphy, resembled him like a brother. The patriotic military were removed. Formerly head of the presidential guard and very close to Jean-Claude Duvalier, Avril was not going to threaten the privileged people. The Catholic hierarchy had no more need of Aristide as a shield. Instead, they denounced liberation theology and the church "that pretends to be from the people" — in short, they renewed their attack on the movement of renewal and its spokespersons. They had burned my church, but, once again, I was a nuisance. The fortunes of politics and of history had transformed me, in their hands, into a ping-pong ball — and as an old school ping-pong player, I knew very well what he was talking about.

The new political situation produced a new verdict: more severe and more brutal. Either I left the country or I left the congregation. Jacques Mésidor tried in vain to intervene, but there was nothing he could do. I sometimes wondered if they did not hope I would leave both the country *and* the congregation! The local Salesians took part in the staging and played the music, but the play itself was written elsewhere, in a concerted move involving the dominant political class, the oligarchy associated with imperialism, the Haitian church, and Rome. The green light could only have been given at the highest level.

The bishops—the majority of the Haitian episcopal conference—had thrown all their weight on the scales: Aristide must not be allowed to carry on his insidious work. He is a dangerous element. Although the threat of exclusion afflicted me deeply, the popular support warmed my heart. The worker and peasant organizations, the youth movements, the women's movement, priests singly or in groups, and even the international associations protested, demanding that the Haitian bishops intervene. It is hard to imagine the majority of the bishops coming to my aid!

On the eve of the verdict, I called for everyone to keep calm. I expressed my deeply felt thanks for the aid and support I had received from every direction.

In a radio talk on November 22, 1988, two months after the coup, I summarized many of the people's objections to the situation in Haiti:

> To my sisters, my brothers,
> To all my brothers and sisters in the Good Lord
> Who raise their voices together with us,
> To the valiant youth of Haiti,
> To the peasants—whether Catholic, Protestant, or
>   Vodouisant—
> To the brave Haitians abroad,
> To the courageous Haitians here in Haiti,
> And to all of you who have just achieved a legal
>   general strike

In spite of the declarations of an illegal general:
Hats off to you,
Congratulations on your courage.

Courageously, you stand up, and you speak.
Courageously, you stand up, and you do not give
     way. I see all this.
I see you speaking for the Lord.
I hear the Lord's voice in your voice.
I am watching you rise up here and abroad
So that I may be permitted to stay with you here
     in Haiti
—and to be with you who are abroad.

A beautiful inspiration from the Holy Spirit!
A beautiful declaration of brotherly love, a dec-
     laration
Which invites me to look you in the eye, my sisters
     and brothers,
And to say to you what Jesus would have said to
     you
In his language: *Ani ohev otha, ani ohev ota'kh.*
I love you.

You who have plotted against me,
You who have plotted against the Haitian people:
Bishop Paolo Romeo, Bishop Gayot, Bishop
     Ligondé,
Bishop Kebreau and the rest,
Let me look you in the eye,
Please, don't be ashamed.
Look me in the eye.
I have come to tell you: I love you, too.
Because I love you, I must tell you the truth.
Truth and love are the same.
Truth and love are Jesus in the midst of the poor.

What luck for the Haitian church,
Rich, thanks to the poor,
In a country that is poor because of the rich.
The church is rich, thanks to us, the poor,
Who ceaselessly demand the truth
From every corner.

What luck for the Haitian church,
Rich, thanks to the poor,
In a country that is poor because of the rich.

The church is rich, thanks to us, the poor,
Who have stopped certain bishops
(Hidden behind the sins they commit)
When they try to tell lies,
To conspire together
And to create silence.

What luck for the Haitian church,
Rich, thanks to the poor,
In a country that is poor because of the rich.

The church is rich, thanks to us, the poor,
Who have agreed to be part of one sole body
In order to avoid the monolith of a head without
    a body.

Alone, we are weak.
Together, we are strong.
Together, we are the flood.

Let the flood descend, the flood of
Poor peasants and poor soldiers,
The flood of the poor jobless multitudes (and poor
    soldiers),
Of poor workers (and poor soldiers),
The flood of all our poor friends (and all the poor
    soldiers) and

The church of the poor, which we call the children
   of God!
Let that flood descend!
And then God will descend and put down the
   mighty and send them away,
And God will raise up the lowly and place them
   on high (cf. Luke 1:52).

To prevent the flood of the children of God from
   descending,
The imperialists in cassocks have conspired with
   the imperialists of America.
This is why we Haitians must say to one another
   what Jesus declared (Mark 2:11):
Arise! Go forth! Walk!

Yes, arise and go forth. Walk.
Arise and go forth so that the Tontons Macoute
   will stop walking in ways wet with our blood.
Arise and go forth so that the criminals will stop
   walking upon us.
Arise and go forth so that the assassins will stop
   waking us in our beds with rounds of gunfire.

Too much blood has been spilled!
Too many of the innocent have fallen!
This is too much for us.

General Avril, you have said: Haiti is debased.
And then? And then nothing!
You said you would close the infamous prison,
   Fort Dimanche.
And then? And then, nothing!
The people are hungry. Misery inhabits their
   bones. Your arms are turned against them.
Wait! you say to the people.

The workers are in trouble. The schools are falling
   apart. The universities are in shreds.
Wait! you say.

The peasantry is trapped with nowhere to go. But
   the rural sheriffs are doing just fine.
Just hold on! you tell the people. Why are you all
   in such a hurry? you ask them.

St. Jean Bosco burned to the ground. Franck
   Romain on the prowl.
Mr. Avril supporting him.
Wait! says Avril to the people.

The little boss is on the payroll of the big boss.
   The big boss is on the Americans' payroll.
Ah, ah, ah. . . . Wait! you tell us.

I'm trying to fix this car, General Avril says.
I'm trying to fix it, and then you all come along
   and stick your hands in the engine. You're going
   to get hurt, he tells us.
Just sit back and wait! Avril says.

Slavery in the Army.
Slavery in the Dominican Republic.
Too bad! you say to the people. Just wait a little.

One coup d'état. Another coup d'état.
One general goes. Another takes his place.
And then? And then, nothing!

Wait?
Until when?
Until the cows come home and pigs fly.

General Avril,
the people's court is right:

Your government is guilty and powerless.
You are guilty
  because you have allowed the savage Tontons
  Macoute to run wild
with no cord of justice around their necks.
You are guilty
  because you have refused to tie the cord of justice around the necks of Franck Romain and
  the other men who massacre.
You are guilty
  because you betray the soldiers who brought you
  to power,
  because you discharge patriotic soldiers,
  because you protect corrupt soldiers.

You are guilty
  because before justice is done, you want to send
  the people to die in sham elections, just to satisfy the American government.

You are guilty
  because you are playing François Duvalier's
  game.

You are powerless
  because your government gets:
Zero points for justice;
Zero points for public security;
And only one point for clean-up—you got rid of
  Namphy.

General Avril, can't you see that the train that
  derailed Namphy is going to go off the tracks
  even faster with you if, before November 29, you
  do not:
Free the patriotic soldiers, arrest the Macoutes,
Lock up Franck Romain, clean out corruption,
And end insecurity in the streets?

The matter is in your hands.
The people will write their own fate.
The blessing of God is upon them. Thus, grace will
    descend until the flood brings down
All Duvalierists,
All Macoutes,
All criminals,
Forever and ever.
Amen.

I knew in what part of the church the oppressed were gathered together, and in light of that knowledge my doubts disappeared and were replaced by a new determination. I had signed up for the battle of the millennium, the rebellion against fatalism, the refusal to abdicate or give up. Yes, to be Christian is to be a rebel. Those who denounced religion as an opium for the people actually helped religion. It cannot be anything other than a battle against resignation; otherwise religion itself must be resisted. When religion does not defend human beings, it must be resisted. When a bishop blesses the cannon—I remember how it was in the Vietnam War—or when he supports generals who murder liberty, he commits a crime.

Two weeks before Christmas 1988 the verdict came down, this time without appeal. I was expelled from the Salesian order. The decree for the dismissal of Father Aristide stated that "his attitude has had a negative effect on his confrères . . . his selfishness demonstrates a lack of sincerity and of a religious and priestly consciousness." The judgment indicates "the impossibility of a sincere and fruitful dialogue, . . . incitement to hatred and violence, and a glorifying of class struggle, . . . the profanation of the liturgy. . . . Father Jean-Bertrand Aristide has always preferred to distance himself from the concrete demands of community, becoming a protagonist of the destabilization of the community of the faithful; and he has done so in a constant, public and incisive manner, so that the organs of the press and groups of varied origins present him as the 'leader of the popular church' " in Haiti. . . .

One can manipulate scientific concepts, and one can sometimes legitimately diverge from them or even oppose them. One can also demonstrate bad faith or fall into sheer idiocy. I did not invent class struggle, no more than Karl Marx did. I would even prefer never to have seen it. Perhaps that is possible, if one never leaves the squares of the Vatican or the heights of Pétionville. But who can avoid encountering class struggle in the heart of Port-au-Prince? It is not a subject of controversy, but a fact, a given. As for the best way of reducing that antagonism, the debate is open on that point.

When some doctor of the faith and (or) of business condemns me by shouting "but you are in favor of class struggle"—therefore a bad priest and a bad citizen—I answer that I am neither for nor against it. Nobody is going to organize a referendum to discover whether the law of gravity is good or bad. It all reminds me of the proceedings brought against Galileo to force him to deny the fact that the earth moves. And still, it does move.

These people have tried to change a political debate into a theological problem. When all the democratic groups are outraged and protest against an unjust decision, while the spokespersons of power are silent, I do not worry a great deal about myself. For the Haitian people, I hope to see a May after April.* May—a real springtime.

---

*In French, April is spelled *avril*, the name of the Haitian general.

Maggie Steber

Father Jean-Bertrand Aristide meditating (1987).

Maggie Steber

Father Aristide speaking to the congregation at St. Jean Bosco during a youth protest against the military government (1987).

Maggie Steber

Street orphans—a part of Father Aristide's flock who became the *Lafanmi Selavi* community.

Maggie Steber

Father Aristide speaking to a pro-union demonstration
after the union office was burned (1987).

Maggie Steber

Father Aristide concelebrating Mass after the attack at
Freycineau (1987).

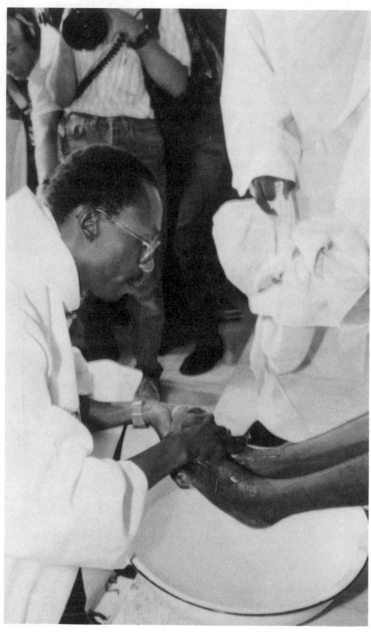

Maggie Steber

Father Aristide washing a peasant's feet at the first Mass after the assassination attempt at Freycineau (1987).

Saving books at St. Jean Bosco after the Macoutes' attack (September 11, 1988).

Maggie Steber

Maggie Steber

Haitians celebrate Mass in the burned-out hulk of St. Jean Bosco (December 1988).

Maggie Steber

Father Aristide comforting a child (December 5, 1990).

Jerry Berndt

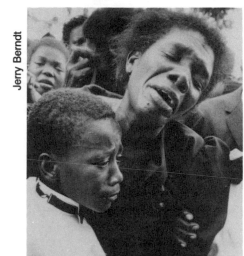

Grieving relatives of the
eight people killed in the
attack at Pétionville
(December 5, 1990).

Jerry Berndt

Spontaneous celebrations of Father Aristide's election
(December 16, 1990).

Jean-Bertrand Aristide, installed as President of Haiti (February 7, 1991).

CHAPTER 9

The Election Drum

Even if class antagonisms were not less sharp in Haiti, even if the world was still turning through the second post-Duvalier dictatorship, history continued to move forward all the same, sometimes stealthily, sometimes at a quick pace. Our strategy remained the same: to rally the exploited, to denounce the dictatorship, to refuse to respond to its daily violence with violence of our own, and to dedicate ourselves to stopping it whenever it occurred. The rifles and the cannon were always on the same side.

I have often been asked about my relationship to people as different as Gandhi and Martin Luther King: remarkable people, genuine prophets of struggle, in a class I will never attain, and fighting for a long time, a very long time against the same enemy, but under other skies. Both were killed by assassins, the one among the wretched of the earth, the other surrounded by the wealth of a majority who oppress their slaves. I do not aspire to martyrdom. Those heroes were not my contemporaries, but my strategy is the same as theirs: nonviolence. Nonviolence is collective resistance, not resignation.

The gospel demands it. I very quickly discovered the congruence between the attitude of Jesus and nonviolence: his way of loving his enemies, his way of giving dignity to the outsiders, of pardoning those who injured him, of speaking a word of truth whether it was pleasant or not—all these things harbor an unbelievable power. Others besides Christ have laid claim to that power of love and truth to turn back violence, hatred, falsehood and injustice, for nonviolence is the common property of humanity. It belongs to everyone, whether believers or not.

To the long list of martyrs, I might have added Oscar Romero, the archbishop of San Salvador, assassinated by the death squads, Chico Mendes and so many other South Americans who died of the same bullets. How could I name all those whose path has sketched my own? Let me mention just one more: a true prophet, a saint of our times who is living still—Dom Helder Camara, the former archbishop of Recife. He is a true disciple of Christ, a man always in communion with the people, the *braceros* and the people of the *favellas*, a man whom the system can never corrupt.

The church could have made a man like that pope, since he is one of their best. They never dreamed of it. So much the better! The system is so close to the world's compromises, so deeply implicated in the twists and turns of diplomacy that Dom Helder Camara would have lost his prophetic purity there, and watered down the uncompromising force of his words. This bishop, as someone engaged in the front ranks of the popular movement, is more than an example: he is a lesson that is permanent and always up-to-date, a cautionary sign for my meditation, not only today, but tomorrow as well.

The year 1989 marked the two hundredth anniversary of the Declaration of Human Rights. It was more than an anniversary: we were about to witness a marvelous new beginning, its impulse coming from Europe. The failure of the totalitarian regimes in the Old World was translated into a tremendous push toward democratic freedom: above all, a victory for humanity! It was a victory or an encouragement for all those who had invested and are investing their energy on behalf of nonviolent action, in the service of justice, peace, and democracy.

The good news? It was that human liberation does not

necessarily occur through violence. As Jesus said, it is possible to struggle for justice and peace without hating and without killing—even if the church of yesterday or today has turned away from the gospel message of nonviolence, even if it has willingly confused that message with a call for resignation. Having taken the side of power, it has often placed itself on the side of violence as well.

The tumult of world events reached as far as Port-au-Prince, although the echoes were muffled by distance. It took longer for 1989 to strike a spark here than in Warsaw or Berlin: in fact, we had to wait for 1990!

Avril was, of course, governing for the benefit of the same people—his past guaranteed that—but he had to work hard to maintain a throne that his own friends were seeking with a fierce appetite. Careerism, egotism, and nepotism set the various clans against one another, and they struggled savagely behind the white facade of the National Palace. Their greed bordered on cannibalism.

The army itself was not as united as Avril would have wished. How could he re-establish a semblance of social harmony when he was busy trying to prevent or checkmate the various attempts at rebellion, even within the one institution on which he should have been able to rely.

The result was a week of attempts to settle accounts. These took place in the city during the month of April and had, as their characteristic result, an intensification of the condemnation and repression of the democratic movement.

Let there be no doubt: my expulsion from the Salesians had not changed my Christian conscience, blunted my fidelity to the dispossessed, or cooled the burning questions I addressed to the Catholic hierarchy. Some people expected that I would join a political party—of which there was already a very rich spectrum, even on the left—or, better still, that I would start my own. That would only have given credibility to the accusations uttered here and there about my immoderate taste for power, a power that, according to others, I wanted to acquire at any price.

Nevertheless, there was an obvious disruption of my daily life, although it was surely more obvious to me than to my friends. I no longer lived with the Salesians, and this constituted the breakup of a marriage that had lasted more than fifteen years. Paradoxically, the *Ti legliz* had never been closer to me.

St. Jean Bosco, battered by criminals, was more alive than ever. It was even radiant: the Christian community gathered in the ruins, more often than before, more numerous than usual. I no longer visited the place, so as not to give the impression that I was trying to hang on there, that I was indispensable or, on the contrary, that I could not exist without it. My desire, rather, was to expand the struggle, and I encouraged the people to extend and enrich the life of their community. Alone, they gathered around the gospel and celebrated their liberating faith. No one could pretend that they were the victims of an agitator. They assumed their responsibilities, taking the measure of their own power. Here was a people without a priest, a numerous people on a road leading toward a collective priesthood! They were fully aware of it — they said the Mass, and said it in the ruins where the martyrs had fallen. It was the same struggle that was still going on.

When they celebrated the eucharist, of course, they modified the ritual and the rhythm, but the heart of religion is not the liturgy. They did not take bread and call it the body of Christ, but they read the gospel, chewed the bread of the word, shared their reflections, sang and prayed.

This is the practice of liberation theology, a tide that cannot be stopped by burned churches, by muzzled priests, by fallen martyrs or the constant repetition of threats, and which swells with the experiences and events lived every day by each and every one.

The political demand of the hour remained the same: to *dechouker* (topple) the usurping general, while seeing to it that he not be replaced by another apprentice dictator, military or not. In the face of the crumbling of political parties, the lack of reliable elections in the near future, how could an alternative be defined? Avril had, in fact, partially restored the constitution of 1987, but that was nothing but a lure that was not likely to catch any political fish.

At the least challenge, the man in power, under pressure even from within his own government, responded with intimidation and repression. He was prepared to escalate matters all the way. He was particularly furious at the media, which he wanted either to control or to eliminate. One could never adequately acknowledge the role of the press, especially the radio, to which everyone listened, or the newspapers that sometimes defied the censors, in informing the Haitian people. Hence Avril's spitefulness and that of his cronies against journalists, who were always confused with militants. To be an honest journalist in Haiti implied being considered a rebel by those in power.

Many of my friends spoke on Radio Soleil, a station that was dependent on the episcopacy, but whose tone was less soothing or less complacent than that of some of our prelates. The latter caved in to the dictator again. So as not to displease the generals, the Catholic hierarchy dismissed the staff of Radio Soleil. Again they succumbed to the criminal illusion that it is possible to win over the wielders of bayonets by giving in to them!

I do not know whether those in power, in their use of intimidation or psychological warfare, were drawing their inspiration from South American dictatorships or from those of eastern Europe (the latter now in disarray), but they went beyond their work of November 2, 1989. This was not evident in the number of dead, for there were none this time and the previous record would have been difficult to surpass in any case—but in the level of baseness, cynicism, and, finally, stupidity.

Three leaders of popular organizations, three militants known to everyone, were complacently shown on television. They had first been beaten up: the marks of the blows were visible. Étienne Marine, Jean-Auguste Mesyeux, the executive secretary of CATH, and Evans Paul, all opponents of

Duvalierism from the beginning, were accused of high treason. They were said to be the instigators of an armed plot intended to overthrow the government of General Avril. (What a legitimate aim!) Worse, according to their prosecutors, they were preparing to assassinate all the generals. We were living out one of the fables of La Fontaine, a new version of "The Animals Infected with the Plague." The criminals absolve themselves and pardon the other criminals, but they are ready to reduce to silence — i.e., to eliminate — the authors of crimes of opinion. Would the fable again turn into a nightmare?

This time the reaction was spontaneous, massive, the mirror image of the brutal and impudent blunder of the military. The result was a series of general strikes and hunger strikes in unison with and in solidarity with the prisoners. International opinion became involved, never a negligible factor if one is aware of the financial vulnerability of the generals and the aptitude of their Macoute friends for robbing the treasuries that had been temporarily filled by foreign aid.

Avril bent, but he tried again on January 20, 1990. Like his predecessors, he reflected the assurance that fear governs everything, and that terror exercised on a few would produce good behavior on the part of the many. The contagion of fear had been the essential resource of Duvalierism. Was it still enough? The faithful at St. Jean Bosco were moving toward their church, which they knew to be in danger. The strikers streamed along the streets in spite of beatings and gunfire. Disobedience spread across the country like a massive oil spill.

At the ecumenical Center for Human Rights, opposition leaders were being arrested as fast as possible: more than thirty people, all of them savagely beaten. Then, to complete the fishing expedition, the leaders of the opposition were picked up at home: Max Bourjolly, Serge Gilles, Hubert de Ronceray, and many others. At that time I kept changing my residence, since it was dangerous to sleep under the same roof for several nights in a row.

For good measure, the government suspended the constitution, established censorship and decreed a state of siege: all of this was intended to "legalize" practices that had become quite ordinary. But fear did not create more fear, and terror did not breed more terror. Avril was more and more isolated in a bleeding country where public services were barely functioning, where the schools were closed, and the financial backers became more and more impatient. He found himself face to face with a determined and unified opposition. The organizing assembly, which coordinated the twelve principal organizations, left them no choice. It demanded his immediate and unconditional resignation from office and the formation of a provisional government headed by a member of the Supreme Court of Appeals and a Council of State of twenty members representing all sectors of Haitian society.

The ultimatum was issued on March 4, 1990; on the 10th, Avril resigned. General Hérard Abraham recalled the army to its barracks and took power only in order to surrender it quickly to the provisional government. Ertha Pascal Trouillot became provisional president until the elections. Elections! Would we have real elections, as we had been promised: free, clean, honest, protected against any kind of manipulation, before the end of the year?

The appearance of Ertha created a certain amount of hope and a good deal of suspicion, since the politico-military class had accustomed us to conjuring tricks, sometimes bloody, given that the bourgeoisie was little inclined to surrender its share of political power to the people. The Council of State was a collection of good people, honest personalities, some of them well known, but there were no militants directly associated with the daily struggles against the dictatorships.

They were ready to collaborate with Ertha, although no one was sure that she really wanted these elections. It was true that she talked about them all the time, but Namphy had also announced elections with some regularity. Like him, she was afraid of any kind of popular interference. The competence and honesty of the Council of State — sometimes bordering on naïveté in dealing with the executive — led me later to demand that our own should have a third qualification: experience with militancy.

These two organs — the provisional government and the Council of State — could not agree, with the result that the executive was paralyzed. Ertha showed no eagerness to pursue the accomplices of the dictatorship, the organized gangs: that is, the barons of Macoutism. She temporized. To hold elections without security, without justice and without respect for the previous victims: would that be possible or acceptable?

The people demanded the arrest of the Duvalierists who were parading about the city: in short, they called for a political cleanup, for acts of purification that were not solely economic in nature. There were old Macoutes shamelessly announcing their candidacies! Elections would only be acceptable after the killers and their accomplices had been arrested. One part of the popular movement pressed for this prior demand. There could be no question of giving in or of being associated with a November 29 revisited — or something worse!

I found myself once again among those opposing the people in power. That whole summer I tried to sensitize opinion, especially on the international level, regarding the obstacle in the way of future elections: the need, beforehand, to pass judgment on those who had massacred the peasants, those who had burned St. Jean Bosco, the machine-gunners of November 29, to mention only the worst of them. Beyond that, what guarantees did the army offer, even if General Abraham had behaved loyally in March? He was not alone, in an institution so accustomed to intervening in the political sphere.

The arrival of Roger Lafontant in Haiti in June gave me an additional reason to be uneasy. Lafontant! He was one of the most notorious of the Macoutes, a zealous servant of the regime, Minister of the Interior and of Defense, both together, since 1972. It is a serious accusation to say that a man has blood on his hands. In this case, it is a euphemism. The chief of the death squads, one of the men most closely associated with every kind of torture and killing, was moving about freely. He enjoyed a calm impunity, despite the fact that he had been forbidden to enter Haiti and, at the same time, that a warrant had been issued for his arrest. Part of the army assured him of peace, assistance and protection.

How could Ertha tolerate such a provocation? Apparently without much surprise or disquiet. There was a subtle ballet in which the game consisted of tossing a ball back and forth, keeping it as briefly as possible before throwing it to someone else. The executive should not get mixed up in the administration of justice: the separation of powers demands this. The judge returns the ball to the commissioner: the army cannot carry out the judgment; that is the duty of the police. And the police have no orders! Ertha ignored the problem while the oligarchy laughed, and so did Lafontant. Would we be trapped in the vicious circle, so easily closed? Were we about to be the victims, the donkey in the fable, once again?

In the streets of Port-au-Prince, the mafiosi had resumed their usual activities. They occupied their summer quarters in tranquillity. The interim president, who was piling up more and more incidents between herself and the Council of State, seemed to be willing to put up with them. The date of the elections was postponed. Was time being provided for the neo-Duvalierists to organize?

The date was set for December 16, 1990. A president and members of parliament were to be elected. But what kind of elections would the Haitian people witness or take part in? Would they be elections by machete and machine gun, the voters discouraged or forced to vote at gunpoint—or would the ballot boxes be stuffed? In spite of protests, petitions, and strikes, Lafontant had been in the country for three months. The balloting was set for three months in the future. And then, on October 16, the Union for National Reconciliation, a new party with unlimited means, announced the candidacy of its leader, Roger Lafontant.

The political reality, still as dangerous, was becoming clearer for me, and for others as well. Our political thinking had to make a decisive shift. We had always asked how we could beat the drum of elections without beating the drum of justice? But we were threatened with division. You can't eat your soup with a fork, as we say in Creole. The proverb had become *"fouchèt divizyon pa bwè soup eleksyon."* In other words, we could not go on eating our electoral soup with a fork!

We were in danger of falling into a trap. The executive, no doubt egged on by imperialism, was trying to keep the people at a distance from the electoral scene. By moving toward a boycott or toward more radical measures, we would cede the ground to others, to some Manigat who would be more easily elected and more solidly entrenched in power. The fact was that international opinion demanded these elections, and in any event Ertha was not Namphy. Letting the Macoutes roam around and be active was not necessarily putting them in the saddle, but it put pressure on the people to abstain from voting and to allow the bourgeoisie alone to choose among acceptable candidates.

The impunity accorded the Macoutes was a tactic; the multiplication of opposition parties and candidates left scarcely any chance for the left. The winner might be a conservative who was not too badly compromised, supported by Ertha, by the privileged, and by Uncle Sam, and international opinion would applaud the conclusion of the crisis and the elimination of one of the most shameful warts in the Americas.

One part of the bourgeoisie wanted to restore the dictatorship for its own profit. It made some changes in the outer shell, which was unacceptable both to the Haitians and to foreigners, by lending it the appearance of democracy. The result of our electoral boycott would be a formal system that would eliminate all the lower classes. We would ultimately concede to the bourgeoisie a limited suffrage that they would not have dared to propose themselves, which would produce an administration without social perspectives, opaque to outside observers, and devoid of justice. Dark forces, relieved of their criminal component, would be able to regain control and perpetuate themselves.

Should we go on killing ourselves? It was certainly necessary to demand the punishment of the Macoutes, and to concede nothing on that point. It was also necessary to achieve unity in the popular movement. And finally, it was necessary to go to the polls.

Since 1985, the Haitian political landscape had been daily enriched with new constellations of groups, associations, and parties with political, social, or humanist ends. Some counted only a few dozen members, while the influence of others did not extend beyond the boundaries of a village or a region. Unity was a *sine qua non* for our participation, and perhaps for our success. These groups, these parties, standing in the breach for such a long time, unceasingly persecuted, were of the same mind. The confluence of rivulets and then of rivers could feed the torrent that would sweep away, along with the old regime, all those who hesitated to renounce it once and for all.

To stop Lafontant was the minimum of justice, the first action of a government worthy of the name. However difficult it might be for me, I no longer considered this a preliminary round. In October, I had had a presentiment of the importance of international opinion. Hundreds of observers, whose probity could not be called into question, would be present. This time, the person elected could boast of a legitimacy almost beyond discussion. Alas for those who were absent!

I expended a lot of energy in fighting against the obstinacy of those opposed to the election, but that did not make the least change in my willingness to have it out with the mafia when the moment came. Let us be as clever as they, let us be aware of the trap, let us respond with unity: how many times did I hammer out these words, all of them summed up in the Creole saying: "*fouchèt divizyon pa bwè soup eleksyon?*"

The idea of my becoming a candidate did not originate in 1990. It had often been proposed to me by my friends, the young people, various groups, readers or hearers. I would be pretending naïveté if I maintained that I had never dreamed of it. I had always refused. I considered my essential role to be that of a consciousness-raiser or spokesperson of the oppressed. I had even declared, a few weeks earlier, at the time when candidacies were being announced—I should say when they were avalanching—that I was inoculated against "presidentialism." If journalists were asking me the question, it implied that the pressures were already strong and many.

Presidentialism is a sickness that "political" doctors can easily find in Haiti. The diagnosis is easy, but the remedy is less sure. Our history is full of that epidemic, the principal symptom of which is a ravenous desire on the part of the patient.

The presidency of Haiti always means power, honor, and money, precisely the reverse of what we were trying to achieve: to be of service to others, and especially to those who are most destitute. But I recognized the situation. I had preached unity, and I remember how my hearers always reacted: "You are asking for an alternative to emerge, a leader who has the complete confidence of the people, and yet you will not agree to be our candidate. You are a coward. Now shut up!" That kind of reaction or thinking was everywhere, and it sometimes made me uneasy. Politicians love so much to say that they have "yielded to the pressing entreaties of their friends," which made these testimonies a torture to me. It was not only my friends; it was a deep and growing movement over which, as God is my witness, I had no control.

The parties of the left, the discussion groups, the conclaves within the assemblies, were working hard to choose a single candidate. These were legitimate but Byzantine discussions in which I did not participate. Nevertheless, the danger was clear, already identified; it even had a name: Lafontant. This fellow, well protected, fully armed, surrounded by gangs of mercenaries, was blowing his own horn to the point of holding a meeting in Vertaillis. The Macoutes gathered with complete impunity and had already passed a death sentence on anyone who dared to run against them. They had clearly asserted that a popular candidate (a communist, of course, according to their vocabulary) would be given a suspended sentence of death.

No name jumped out of the political hat. The messages proposing the candidacy of "Titid," mainly broadcast over the radio, began to multiply and repeat themselves: peasant associations, neighborhood committees, Christian communities, youth movements were heard from. They were all the more anxious to push the movement forward, since on Lafontant's side the politicians were placing a second iron in the fire: the ANDP (National Association for Democracy and Progress), a more centrist version of the Union for National Reconciliation, but the lesser evil in case of failure.

The idea of *lavalas*—the torrent that scours everything in its way—was making progress in public opinion; there was a surge of interest in unity, in making a clean slate of the shameful recent past and totally rooting out Macoutism. The breaking of the wave. *Dechouker*. Rebirth. The National Front for Change and Democracy (FNCD) asked me to clarify my position, to declare myself. The Front, like the other parties, had its own candidate. There was no question of my taking his place without the endorsement of everyone, and without his own agreement. Nor was there any question of my being the candidate of a single party, no matter how close it might be to my own ideas; I could not even represent a group of parties.

These last were so numerous that, in the end, they were of little value. The radicalized Christian communities, the *Ti legliz*, were active in another direction. Would they accuse me of being too rigid or unfriendly if I asserted that the parties only influenced groups that were still limited, embroiled in their own quarrels, too numerous and appealing to widely scattered factions?

The danger of death had little influence on my decision

about being a candidate. That was one of the risks of daily life, a price that other, better people had already paid. My lack of taste for the highest office, my preference for the contest today and vigilance tomorrow, were the things that inclined me to refuse. The people thought of me as a shield, a free and disinterested spokesperson. We had been companions for a long time; we were "twins," as the people said, or "spouses." "*Titid ak pèp la se marasa*" ("Titid and the people are married"). If I were to refuse, they would regard it as a betrayal, as they would have done had I obeyed the orders for my exile in 1987 and 1988, or deferred the Mass at St. Jean Bosco, however gruesome it turned out to be. My candidacy was part of their reflexive self-defense; my place at the heart of the popular movement was reassuring. My program was enough for them: six years of a hard life shared with them.

A long conversation with Father Adrien, my long-term confrère and teacher in so many ways, completed my process of decision. We discussed the matter for a long time. We had served the people together: would we not be betraying them by letting them climb the last steps toward democracy alone? Was political responsibility the extension of the prophetic role of our communities?

The light did not spring up as quickly as electricity when the switch is pressed. I had meditated and prayed: I would accept the responsibility, I would be the candidate of all my companions in misery, known or unknown. It has often been written that I have increasingly regarded myself as a prophet, but I only have the feeling of obeying the word of God and of being the representative of communities that, in themselves, are certainly prophetic. But that kind of definition is secondary: the essential thing is to say what one sees and feels, while remaining oneself.

No, I am not a Messiah, and the population is sane and realistic about that. In our day, there is no Messiah other than the people, no other miracle to be awaited than what is born from dialogue and sincere listening.

If I am a prophet, there are many other prophets besides me. As for miracles, an individual alone will never accomplish anything. Miracles only happen when we are together. *"Pase pou ou kwè nan mirak, pou ou chita ap tan-n mirak, pito ou pa kwè. Men rivé fe mirak, konsa wa vin kwè nan mirak"* ("better not to believe, than to believe in a miracle from heaven!") The miracle is the responsibility of women and men to take control of their future; it is never the simple waiting of a people who are resigned.

If I have any talent as a visionary, I owe it to those who have marched at my side. My vision of politics, like my vision of Christian faith, is fed by others and lives in community. Such a view and such a certainty will permit the people, the community, to continue without me in the future. I am, like everyone else, and perhaps more than some, called to disappear.

Unlike those who see Jesus as a divine being, I discern in him before anything else someone who was fully human. It is out of that human dimension that the divine in him is revealed. He was so human that he was God: I share that theological vision. That is why I finally agreed to discover and experience the complementarity between the priest and the president. If the people can mobilize so much energy for its priest-candidate, it is because they see in him a human being capable of playing a new political role and advancing toward a country characterized by justice, love and respect.

Meanwhile, I announced my candidacy for the presidency of the republic on October 18. It was one more adventure within the remarkable adventure of being human, a wager that was far from being won at the moment when it was laid.

CHAPTER 10

Lavalas

It is certain that my candidacy did not please everyone, and not every Haitian reckoned on the number of my supporters. In five years, the lines of cleavage had scarcely changed at all. As the spokesperson of *Lavalas,* I presented myself, above all, as the anti-Macoute candidate. If the interim president had provided them with more than just a breathing space, the full freedom to maneuver, they knew that, once Titid was elected, justice would be done—with equity and promptitude. They had sentenced me to death, but I would be satisfied to hand them over to justice.

However, the mafia was facing two serious disappointments. In face of the protests that were sweeping the country, the electoral council had rejected the candidacy of Lafontant. It was not a warrant for his arrest, but at least it was a setback.

Of course, the Macoutes were attempting to maintain an atmosphere of terror, probably hoping to replay the coup of 1987 by preventing the vote. Lafontant, the former chief of the Macoutes under Jean-Claude Duvalier, and his friend Claude Raymond, a minister in both Duvalier regimes, certainly had no intention of giving up.

On the other hand, the army, the eternal ally or shield of the Macoutes, resisted all temptations to interfere. Under the orders of General Abraham, they kept quiet and this time made ready to guarantee the orderly process of the election.

This new aspect encouraged me to make optimistic comments a few weeks before the election: "Now we can walk hand in hand with the army; it is a marriage in which each partner should be careful not to betray the other."

Assuredly, the United States was not very likely to bet on Titid. The champions of international law in the Gulf War, they had excluded the possibility of intervening directly in Haiti. If they desired to retain their role as economic mentor, the Americans could no longer support the Macoutes, but they had their own candidate, Marc Bazin, for whom they provided ample support during the electoral campaign. On that side there was no shortage of dollars!

Nor was the apostolic nuncio among the supporters of *Lavalas*. The Vatican, which had ratified all the propositions concurring with my ouster, kept silence this time and manifested a spirit of prudence, even of timidity. Perhaps they had drawn lessons from the past, or perhaps they had realized that by picking on one man they had irritated and infuriated a whole nation, poisoning relations between a popular church and an isolated hierarchy. It may be that the Calvary of St. Jean Bosco had moved them in the end. The appeal against my expulsion from the Salesians had received no response: Bishop Paolo Romeo, usually very eloquent, had put a damper on his diatribes against liberation theology.

The episcopal hierarchy's hostility was softening. Was this hesitation? Realism? If my candidacy offended them, at least this time they avoided preemptory declarations or ultimatums.

The electoral council disqualified half of the candidates, including Lafontant. The mafia was trying to create a noxious atmosphere. In spite of the army's numerous preventive patrols, the people imposed their own curfew. The streets were empty after nightfall; all the people shuttered themselves up at home, trying to avoid any confrontations that could exacerbate the latent tension.

But prudence is not the same thing as fear. In spite of the tragic precedents, the people registered for the election *en masse*, some of them for the first time, and many, I think, because I was a candidate. The international observers did not always notice or understand this, underestimating a phenomenon that would skew their predictions. The new registrants were almost all coming from the hills or from the slums.

Shaken by the events, by hesitations and scruples — my own and those of others — I registered officially on the last day. The filing deadline had been set for October 18 at five P.M. It was all decided the evening before. A few hours were needed to gather the identification materials, forms and pledges required for this kind of undertaking. The electoral council had suggested that I should move about midday, after Lafontant had registered his candidacy during the morning. It was better to avoid a meeting between the two of us.

But the head of the mafia was not content to present his dossier. Armed and solidly surrounded by his henchmen, he set up camp in front of the building that housed the electoral council. I was much more afraid for the crowd that would come with me for friendly support than I was for myself. The confrontation could produce new victims to no purpose, and support the strategy of tension that was being practiced by the Macoutes.

I waited. Minutes and hours went by. It was three o'clock; four o'clock; four-fifteen. I waited at home. The radio was already echoing with the provocation. I telephoned the electoral council once more:

"Can you ask Mr. Lafontant to go away?"

"I do not have the means to do so."

"Could you extend the time for registering a candidacy until six o'clock?"

"No."

"Then could we postpone our meeting until tomorrow morning, in order to avoid any incident?"

"It is not in our power to extend the deadline."

"I am coming then; you will have to accept the responsibility!"

Lafontant and his bullies were gathered at the foot of the steps. There was also a detachment of the army that rushed toward my car. Then it seemed as if I was being abducted, lifted off the ground and carried in the wink of an eye before the electoral council. Those few seconds left me with a memory of being transformed into an airplane or a flying carpet: this metamorphosis was shaped by the solid and affectionate arms of a new form of military transport. My feet went on beating the air all by themselves, while Lafontant's men were rooted to the ground, blocked away by the soldiers. The bandit had not been able to prevent my candidacy. Later, he would swear that he would have been able to prevent the "communists" from plundering Haiti.

Communist! People always tried to use that word like a scarecrow. Our opponents used and abused it. What are we, what am I, if not the crystallization of popular demands, the promise of bread, justice and respect? They would have liked to be able to catalogue me more precisely, to label me, to prove that I drew my inspiration from foreign models: a follower of Fidel Castro, an admirer of the Sandinistas, a fomenter of civil war or coups d'état, an imitator of Salvador Allende or of the Shining Path. I have been compared to Jean-Marie Djibaou, a pastor and Kanaka leader who with wisdom and determination led his people to independence.

Often, these comparisons had only one objective: to create fear. I never stopped repeating throughout the campaign that there are no models, only facts and situations. There was nothing that could be transposed to fit here, no talisman that could be photocopied to solve all our problems. That would be another way, just as pernicious, of believing in miracles.

Certainly it is true that others' experience can clarify our own path, give energy to our creativity or open new horizons. But every reproduction that ignores the popular spirit, the national culture that by definition is unique, leads to bitter disillusionment. The "experts" in cooperation know something about this, and they have often wasted millions when they have insisted on importing projects that are economically unadapted or socially unacceptable.

Rather than searching for models, I prefer to welcome those ideas that rest on the values of beauty, dignity, respect, and love. Che Guevara, a bourgeois, a doctor, an internationalist, certainly incorporated some of those values, as did Allende. They were sincere men, like so many others; they made mistakes, just as I will do. Why should I deny it? I feel more affection and sympathy for them than I do for many others.

The western democracies are more convinced now than ever before that there is only one possible model: their own. Even now, at a distance of two centuries, I continue to feel respect and unbounded admiration for the Declaration of Human Rights of 1789, a universal text and the point of departure for our Haitian history. I do not believe that liberal and parliamentary democracy is in itself the indispensable corollary, the sole result and unique end of the movement for human rights. The democracy to be built should be in the image of *Lavalas:* participatory, uncomplicated, and in permanent motion.

Lavalas represented something quite different from the FNCD (National Front for Change and Democracy). The latter was a collection of a variety of movements and political parties and played the role of a stimulus or spur to action, at the same time that it furnished the legal organization necessary to sponsor my candidacy. *Lavalas* was much, much more: a river with many sources, a flood that would sweep away all the dross, all the after-effects of a shameful past.

Operation *Lavalas* brought together a variety of initiatives and is the living proof of the maturity of our people, their readiness for democracy. It is the lever that will enable us, one day, to stop and to eradicate corruption. Belonging to *Lavalas* is not like taking out membership in a political party, paying one's dues. Instead, it means freely joining a movement that transforms perpetual vassals and servants into free men and women. Once again: *"tout moun se moun"* ("everyone is a human being").

We are all free people. *Lavalas* is the opportunity for each and for all. That is what I kept on repeating in innumerable public meetings, and what many others explained here and there. It was the opportunity for the army, formerly a band of mercenaries, to be united with its people. It was the opportunity for the bourgeoisie to opt for a democratic transition rather than for a violent revolution. It was the opportunity for the church to be reconciled with its people. And it was the people's lever for gaining access to instruction, to bread, and in the future, to work.

Lavalas means being united against the mafia, but also being united in order to build something strong. Together, *"men anpil chay pa lou."* As we so often say in Creole, "one finger is not enough to scoop up your gumbo." It is hard to succeed all by oneself: *"you sel dwèt pa manje kalalou."*

One part of the bourgeoisie was worried about *Lavalas*'s program. Certainly they were concerned about the idea that the privileged should cooperate with any efforts toward solidarity, that a redistribution of wealth, freely discussed, should be put into effect, that we would give more encouragement to investments within the country than outside, and that dignity and security should no longer be the prerogatives of a tiny minority. Another part of the bourgeoisie joined in, without a second thought, and labored alongside the homeless, landless, unemployed, voiceless, with the same spontaneity and determination as was shown by those who, in the past, had enabled us to begin *Lafanmi Selavi*, but to a wholly different degree. Our support went far beyond the narrow limits of our little island. The emigrés contributed in every sense of the word, with their money and their know-how: their contributions went a long way toward equalizing our struggle against opponents with immense financial resources.

I have often been criticized for lacking a program, or at least for imprecision in that regard. Was it for lack of time? — a poor excuse. *"La chance qui passe"* ("the opportunity that is getting away") and *"La chance à prendre"* ("the opportunity to be seized") are two basic texts, long, interesting, but often indigestible and inaccessible to 90 percent of Haitians. In fact, the people had their own program. It did not require a wizard to formalize it after years of struggle against neo-Duvalierism. It was a simple program: dignity, transparent simplicity, participation. Those three ideas could be equally well applied in the political and economic sphere and in the moral realm.

At the risk of annoying certain technocrats, I have always avoided the jargon of the social sciences. One does not set oneself to listen to the people in order to reply to them in incomprehensible terms. Is this populism or demagoguery? It is neither one! Rarely did a candidate promise so little. Moral values? Yes. Commercial values? Very few. I never ceased disputing the value of believing in miracles. The candidate of *Lavalas* could not pull anything out of a magician's hat. The leaders of the movement spread the message to everyone, sometimes with difficulty—we cannot do everything or provide everything tomorrow; we will simply try to move from destitution to poverty. *"Tèt ansanm"* ("All together").

The electoral campaign was brief. Never in the history of Haiti had a political movement drawn such crowds. In the hill country, whole villages were present at the meetings. In the city, there often was not enough room to accommodate all our supporters. The enthusiasm was extraordinary. The people chanted *"Pèp la pa ka lage Titid"* ("The people will not let Titid fall"), or *"Chanje leta: ba li koulè revandikasyon pèp-la"* ("We have to change the state: we will give it the colors of the people's demands").

They reiterated the idea that we were twins. If they suffer, I suffer. If I bear it, they can bear it. Whoever attacks them, attacks me. Whoever wounds them injures me. In that autumn of 1990, everyone was ready to move mountains. The questions asked, the topics raised all revolved around *"Tèt ansanm"* ("all together"), or *"makout pa ladan"* ("the struggle against corruption").

As I travelled through the country, the peasants' determination amazed me. Having been more often in contact with the young people of the slums, I had not fully estimated the evolution of the rural scene. The struggle for education or liberation from slavery assumed a dimension I had not expected. They demanded schools, roads, clinics. ... Communities were no longer being constituted simply for the administration of a particular place, but to dispute the place that had so long been assigned to the peasant masses. Are our peasants archaic? The excesses of the speculators would no longer be tolerated, and the dictates of the city were rejected: the radio, to which everyone listened, short-circuited the big shots with breathless speed.

Lavalas, the extension of the *rache manyok,* broke like a wave over the countryside. Operation *Lavalas* was a great deal more than an electoral campaign; it was an enthusiastic feeling of reunion that roused a people relieved of its fear. It was awakening, vigilance, imagination, and it would ensure democracy and security for the future.

Even if the climate remained oppressive and security uncertain, the mafia, under closer surveillance than it was accustomed to, limited itself to a few isolated assassination attempts and several raids, including the one on MOP (Movement for the Organization of the Countryside), which was supporting me. Lafontant had already proclaimed that there was "an international conspiracy plotting acts of political terrorism and assassinations," which would be falsely attributed to the Duvalierists.

The conspiracy, that is to say, the mafia itself, struck on December 5. I was supposed to speak at Pétionville at two in the afternoon, on my return from Kenscof in the mountains. The crowd was so thick that four hours were scarcely enough to drive fifteen kilometers. The *lavalas* of peasants stopped us everywhere we went. A mob of humanity had been waiting for hours in front of the Guards' house, in the center of the city. After the monster meeting at Cap-Haïtien, such a crowd in a town that was securely bourgeois indicated the victory that was coming.

I had started to speak as usual. A group of individuals, apparently favoring me, was applauding at every pause and trying to clear a path toward me. Philippe, one of my friends, thought them suspicious. While forcing them back, he summarily pushed me into a car. We rolled forward a little way, slowly, for bunches of young people were clinging to the roof of the vehicle. We stopped. The teenagers got down from their perch. We started off again. When we had gone only a few dozen yards, an explosion shattered the night, at the very place where our car had been standing three minutes earlier.

I returned toward Pétionville. It was impossible to try anything. I collected myself for a few minutes in a friend's house. The explosive device had claimed sixty victims, eight of them killed, almost all of them young people. The reaction in the political ranks was almost unanimous this time. Calling once again for the arrest of Lafontant, I decided that last week to suspend all meetings in order to deprive the killers of new targets.

In spite of it all, election observers and initial polls in Haiti predicted unanimously that we would win the elections in the first balloting . . . if nothing prevented it from taking place.

On December 16, 1990, I was elected president of the republic. The cock, the bird that sings and rouses, the symbol of *Lavalas,* received two-thirds of the votes. I would begin my duties on February 7, 1991, five years to the day after the flight of Jean-Claude Duvalier.

Several weeks intervened between the election and my installation in office, just long enough to read the files — some of them much more urgent than others — to get an idea of the ruinous state of the public treasury, and to make provisions for the future government; above all, it provided time to picture the forms of popular participation that would extend operation *Lavalas.* Ertha continued to provide stability in the interim.

I had not expected that my first worry would come from the church. Certainly, my case with the Roman authorities stretched into eternity. The appeal against my expulsion, my defense and explanation of the theology of liberation had provoked no response.

Bishop Pétion-Laroche had already asked me fraternally, in the name of canon law, to resign from the priesthood since I had gone into politics full time. At that time I simply promised to avoid any conflict with the Vatican. Later, in company with Bishop Gayot, he insisted that I resign before February 7, the day of my inauguration. Our meeting was very cordial. We agreed to prepare a document addressed to the people, and I was prepared to add my signature to theirs. But Bishop Gayot broke his promise by immediately announcing that I had asked to resign. Were relations with the bishops going to be continually in doubt because of misunderstandings?

After this, a document arrived that took no account whatever of our conversation. I returned the copy with the grade it deserved: zero. This was followed by a new, written proposal to which I was about to give a similar mark when, on January 1, 1991, the archbishop of Port-au-Prince charged into the breach. From his cathedral he launched an incredible salvo of cannon balls against my election. The balloting, which had received the blessing of international observers, was interpreted by Archbishop Ligondé as the Haitian people's descent into hell.

"Fear is sending a chill down the spines of many fathers and mothers of families," he began. Civil liberties were about to disappear; we were heading for "an authoritarian political regime" with the installation of "a political police" and "a campaign of denunciation." "Is socialist Bolshevism going to triumph?" The friend of the Duvaliers, the man who had officiated at Jean-Claude Duvalier's wedding, was fearful for our liberties!

The homily, sprinkled with quotations from Pope John Paul II, presented an apocalyptic vision of Haiti. Ligondé predicted that "in the year 2000 we will be eating stones, and in the year 2004 we will celebrate the centenary of national independence in a desert. . . . Fortunately, a woman is watching over us: Holy Mary, the mother of God." The archbishop, who had criticized me twenty times over for "acting politically," was himself, beyond any doubt, calling even Mary herself to his aid against the 70 percent of Haitians who had just voted for *Lavalas.*

Was he speaking with the endorsement of his fellow bishops? I do not think so. But I very much doubt that he took the initiative on his own, without any support from the other side of the Atlantic. Let me simply say that if Rome had not encouraged him, it did not disown him either. Perhaps there was fear in high places of an alliance between *Lavalas* and the Sandinista movement, which had been supported by priests. They were so very anxious to find models to fit us, and so eager to see us following in someone else's footsteps in order that they might more easily accuse us of anarchism or Bolshevism.

One week later, Ligondé's admonition revealed its full dimensions. This was more than a reprimand; it was the first act of a concerted plot. Lafontant was preparing to play Act Two. The first man pumped up the ideology, thus preparing the ground for the second, who would occupy it with his accustomed brutality.

On the evening of January 6, 1991, Jean-Claude Duvalier's former minister and his militia made an assault on the presidential palace. That night, Lafontant announced that he had assumed full power, erasing at a stroke the presidential election of December, and hoping that part of the army would leap to his side. But that did not happen.

I was at home when the coup d'état was announced. At first Lafontant had tried to get around the soldiers who were responsible for guarding me, to persuade them to hand me over. The tape with his voice giving the formal order for my arrest is still available. After that, two commandos got as far as the gate of my house. I was ready to assume my responsibility as the elected president in the midst of my friends and the loyal soldiers. We were ready for war.

The constitution authorizes keeping a gun at home for use in legitimate cases of self-defense. I would never have thought of it for myself, but to have a gun at hand did not seem to me, in a similar case, to contradict a biblical reading of the events. I have never had a gun, but if it should one day become necessary for me to use one in defense of the poorest of the poor against the powerful forces of organized crime, I would not let myself be paralyzed by the fatalist sentiment of an insipid theology. I have already made my choice between violence and cowardice, even if I would qualify the retort of a legitimate defense by placing violence and cowardice in the same camp. When I think of the Macoutes, I know that they are both cowardly and violent. If there is any risk of an uncertain outcome in a fight, they run away. For them, there is no question of meeting an opponent on equal terms—their cowardice is expressed by their violence.

Lafontant retreated into the palace, where he was quickly isolated by a popular uprising. He had not foreseen Act Three of the play he was acting. At the announcement of the coup d'état, tens of thousands of people had run into the streets, setting up barricades, isolating and surrounding even the presidential palace. At the sound of the *lanbis* (long horns with a deep tone) in an atmosphere suffocating with burning tires, the capital responded in its own way to the proclamation of the one-day dictatorship.

The army, as well as the Western embassies, followed the popular uprising. After a half hour's exchange of gunfire, Lafontant gave himself up. There was already a human carpet occupying the airport to prevent him from fleeing. Ligondé, however, managed to decamp a few hours before the archbishop's house and the nunciature were sacked.

I have often been criticized for the violence of the popular reaction and for the *dechoukajes*. I never encouraged them. They will disappear as soon as the roots of the violence have been *dechoukées*, and when justice is done.

We had been on the verge of civil war. If the army, or its most mercenary part, had supported Lafontant as they did

Namphy or Avril, the capital and the whole country would have been thrown into a merciless civil war. The people were no longer afraid of the Macoutes. Many of them had exhausted their whole store of patience. Every kind of exorcism and every kind of revenge would have been possible.

My entry into office took place, as planned, on February 7, 1991, in a recovered serenity and shared joy.

CHAPTER 11

May the Peace
of the Dollar
Be with You

Two centuries passed between the first slave revolts and
the second independence. The period from 1791 to 1991 represents a long march in the darkness, two hundred years of
struggle to reach the daylight at last. In fact, in spite of want
and the predatory government, a little light was always burning. Even at its palest it inspired the Haitian people to fashion
structures for survival: a sense of equality, of sharing, an
inventiveness in the face of calamities descending from the
sky and, too often, from other people. Socialism in Haiti is
not a new thing: its practice is rooted in the period of our
first independence.

The people have suffered as much from the wickedness of
their leaders as they did from colonialism. A tiny minority
took their cue from the French and perpetuated slavery in
different forms. They imitated their French predecessors as
apes imitate human beings. They drove out the bad masters,
but they had already learned from them how to pillage, steal,
exploit—in short, to reproduce their domination. Today there
are, even within the Haitian bourgeoisie, imitators of the European bourgeoisie of the nineteenth-century type; but there

135

are also men and women who are prepared to involve themselves in the cause, to share and walk together with the peasants, the uprooted and the excluded. They can be found in *Lavalas*, and in the government.

My first job after February 7, 1991, was to return the army to its role as protector of the country and to suppress the last of the paramilitary groups allied with the mafia. I had chosen to strike at the head of the monster. Everyone knew of the political role played by the general staff, but there was less awareness of the extent to which the institution was poisoned with the gangrene of contraband, especially the traffic in cocaine. How else could one explain the lifestyles of some of the officers? Why should anyone be surprised at the reign of corruption, when it was rotting the whole mechanism of the society?

It was quite a challenge: the democratization of the army, to be carried out as rapidly as possible, passed by a tiny margin. As in the sciences, there were many variables, and there were also some formidable unknowns. But one element was certain: the people had shown the army the way to go, after Lafontant's aborted coup d'état.

Otherwise, we certainly had need of a police force. The structure of the army, apart from individuals, had always had the same purpose: to be on guard against the people and to profit from the surrounding corruption. The first measures we took were directed at that situation.

Establishing a collaboration between the people and the police happened slowly because of the heavy weight of the past. Such collaboration was already showing its usefulness in ridding the society of terrorists (*zenglendos*), the gangsters more or less in cahoots with the mafia, and it was supported by the vigilance of the neighborhood committees. After freedom, the second conquest was security: progressive, still fragile, but indispensable.

As for the army, it had to be professionalized and allowed to be of service. That indicates the point at which it had to break with its old habits. Why not have a corps of engineers to help with reforestation, act as a support force for major undertakings and participate in the struggle against certain natural calamities? In that way, the army could reconcile itself with the nation.

The young officers ought to attend the university. In doing so, they would discover possibilities for integrating themselves in society. A new generation, in which women would also have their role, would enable us to break with the past. It was being put into place. Respect for the law, supported by a clear and simple moral code, had already made it possible to limit the extent of corruption in the army, as in the nation itself.

And the Macoutes? The powers of death were still present, with their bullies, their agitators and their arsenals, inside or outside the country. They sometimes struck blindly: a few days before my election, killing four children from *Lafanmi Selavi*; a few weeks later, in the iron market of Port-au-Prince. But arrests were followed by trials. Lafontant himself was condemned to life in prison on July 29, 1991.

I do not think that it was very pleasant to be a Macoute in Haiti any more. But on the other side of the border, there were still some of them, millionaires who had invested a great deal of stolen money in Haiti and therefore benefited from certain protections. They were even able to pay people in Port-au-Prince to shout "Aristide, president for life!" That was one way of discrediting the new order of things. Five years would not be too long to accomplish the clean-up. Even on the margins, Macoutism is like a weed: if you have not dug up all the roots, it will sprout again and insinuate itself into the same structures.

The habit of dictatorship had sometimes produced a kind of Macoutism in people's heads. Tolerance and freedom cannot be learned overnight. But the *dechoukaj*, although less and less frequent, was now inexcusable. In fact, who was really profiting from it now? The democracy that had been flowing in our veins for such a long time, in the form of practice or of rebellion, ought to accustom everyone to accepting the ideas of others. After thirty-five years of dictatorship the power to take full responsibility for oneself as a human being is quite extraordinary!

As a symbol, and as the candidate chosen by the militant movement and by the outsiders themselves, I had to face a flood of delegations, a tide of meetings, and a *lavalas* of requests. Paradoxically, my conversation partners made few demands, but they suggested many changes, offered proposals, and, more than anything, wanted to see the president, as if I could have an answer for everything or be the arbiter of every conflict, like Saint Louis under his oak tree. But I had never thought it would be easy to transform universal suffrage, even when supported by a mass movement, into active citizenship.

The ministers were certainly better informed or more competent than I to respond or to decide. But I had to receive people, give directions, explain that a participatory democracy is a pyramid set on its base and not balancing uneasily on its apex. Once more, I had to point out that it is not I who am the prophet, but the national community itself, growing out of an immense number of living communities.

Regarding that community, I hoped that no one would remain outside. We had to grasp the fleeting opportunity. The bourgeoisie exercised a particular responsibility. They were in possession of a large share of knowledge and ability, as well as capital; they had been favored by the luck of the draw. I invited them to participate in the movement of renewal, to invest in Haiti, and to open a dialogue with the other social strata.

In a real situation shot through with exploitation, flagrant injustices and crimes, everyone had suffered deformation. It was necessary that the privileged of yesterday should learn to respect the whole of society, to act differently, and to take their cue from essential human values. Oppression, beatings, prison: all that was finished. Did everyone understand the necessity to work for himself or herself and for the good of the whole community? We could not renew the use of force, except against the tricksters. Dialogue was already making possible some initial progress toward solidarity. But passive resistance gave birth to new dramas. One part of the bourgeoisie was strongly engaged in the *Lavalas* movement. I had spoken of the patriotic bourgeoisie and the patri*pocket* bourgeoisie. I know that the majority of the latter were too strongly allied with the system of corruption to be recoverable right away.

On May 1, 1991, I warned against mad egoism and economic parasitism, and in severe tones, because they had refused the hand extended to them by the other social strata—they, who had taken refuge in a pathological submission to dictatorship. I had suggested an alliance between bourgeois capital and the revolutionary capital of *Lavalas*, in order that a new economic order might bloom. Before concluding, I said, without losing my sense of humor: "Your dollar will live in peace; may the peace of the dollar be with you. Your dollar will live in peace; may the fear of peace withdraw *lavalassement* from you!"

The bourgeoisie should have been able to understand that its own interest demanded some concessions. We had recreated 1789. Did they want, by their passive resistance, to push the hungry to demand more radical measures? *"Pèp la wonfle jodi-a li kapab gwonde demen"* ("the people that are snoring today can roar tomorrow")! Did the "patripockets" want to see a '93 follow '89? When the people grow impatient, they will not point the finger at the president or the leaders of *Lavalas*, but at those who are getting rich over their backs.

I was ready to take the necessary time to encourage everyone to bathe without hesitation in a disinfected atmosphere that excluded parasitism. I tried to play the social doctor, to convince everyone that the head of the Haitian state was as responsible as the head of a family, that I would prefer to prevent conflicts, but that I would continue at a rapid pace to install a just government whose laws would apply equally to everyone. The political mutation was accomplished without armed force. The social revolution remained to be accomplished. Neither the one nor the other could mean that postelectoral blank checks would circulate in a laissez-faire atmosphere.

"Justice, transparency, participation" was the slogan of *Lavalas*. In moving from opposition to power, something that was not easy either for the ministers or for the militants who had been brought up during the decades of dictatorship, it was necessary for us to create a public administration that was no longer a sinecure, but rather a service, one that served the people instead of using them. This system was gradually put into place with the aid of various organizations, and according to three criteria: competence, militancy, and honesty.

We have sometimes been reproached for being slow in concrete matters. Apart from the fact that this accusation was quite often unjust, with the local collectives giving remarkable demonstrations of imagination (although we had to deal with day-to-day management), we were pressed, even submerged by urgent matters: the appropriation of uncultivated lands, the removal of unscrupulous officials, dealing with the insufficiency of food in certain regions, the revolts of soldiers against certain brutal officers, sabotage by the Macoutes, the conditions under which Haitians in the Dominican Republic were living ... the tally could blacken entire pages, like a Rabelaisian list or a catalogue in the style of Prévert.

How could we entrust funds to administrations and organs that had not yet been renewed? We have been accused rather often of having sometimes refused to extend credits because the local administration was not yet secure from corruption. Thus the minister of social affairs preferred to suspend several cooperative projects as long as the programs within the department remained tainted. As the press could have explained, this illustrated the degree to which the Haitians are viscerally dedicated to the elimination of corruption. As we have seen, drugs were passing through our country without hindrance, for the profit of a few people. We could not get rid of the traffic overnight. But, in collaboration with America and without the least hesitation, we caught several intermediaries red-handed. The task was all the more urgent since the battle with the drug traffickers went hand in hand with our intention to eliminate the mafia structures. The Macoutes and the dealers were often the same people.

With *Lavalas*'s rise to power, Haiti had grown greater, extending far beyond its 27,000 square kilometers and nine departments. Even before February 7, we had created a tenth department encompassing our compatriots outside, who had multiple roles. Without them, what would become of some of the families on the island? Some began to invest, bringing us their competencies and returning to the country regularly or for good. More than a fifth of the population was culturally or economically bonded to their mother country from which they had previously been forced to flee.

Honorary ambassadors of Haiti, ties between the mother country and the rest of the world, enthusiastic supporters of renewal, the avant garde of a new definition of citizenship: they were our pride, the symbol of reunion and communion centering on hope and sharing, from New York to Paris, from Montreal to Miami. Certainly, we offered them their rights and they offered us their interest and the respect that they showed to their brothers and sisters. Thus all the good will was channeled into *"Voye Ayiti monte"* ("Help Haiti Go Forward"), the expression of national pride.

Everyone could come back, temporarily or forever. Everyone came—because Haiti is their country, because they wanted to see how the dictatorship had held the country for ransom, and how they could participate in its reconstruction. There were some who were precious to us because of the skills they had acquired in other countries, where their energies had found soil in which to bloom and grow. Creating a moral state meant purifying its administration. Many Haitians returning from North America made an opportune offer of their services.

After years spent abroad, people returned when they wanted to and when they could, for they knew that, whatever they decided, this country is as much theirs as mine. What we had suffered here they knew and had lived also. They were no longer exiles.

Many millions of dollars had been collected to save the country from three scourges: illiteracy, malnutrition, and deforestation. *Voye Ayiti monte* had set its goal at ten dollars per month per inhabitant.

This natural movement for change, once given life, continued to expand systematically. Such an opening, a movement of cooperation understood in this way, prevented nationalism from turning in on itself; instead it opened itself to Haitians from outside and, naturally, to their host countries. A new citizenship was being forged, together with a new society that cooperates with its branches overseas—what the Greeks called colonies, in a sense far removed from the one to which we have been subjected for two centuries.

At the same time, we could no longer tolerate the unspeakable banishments, the flagrant violations of the most elementary rights that were the lot of Haitians in the Dominican Republic. The government of that country had to come to realize that the very recent era in which Jean-Claude Duvalier had sold Haitians like a gang of slaves had been overturned. Never again would our sisters and brothers be exported like merchandise, their blood changed into bitter sugar.

But a country that has suffered so much disaster needs aid and cooperation on a still greater scale. I willingly employ those two words, aid and cooperation, since it is true that the Haitian people understand how to refine their definition, as well as the forms they will take. We have not reclaimed our dignity within Haiti in order to accept any kind of subjugation that may come from without! As with the long political struggle of the past, we will continue to rely on our own strengths! *"Men anpil chay pa lou"* ("When there are a lot of hands the burden is not heavy").

In speaking of cooperation, are we talking about disinterested assistance, gifts based on certain conditions, reparations, partnerships, investments? If it is a matter of *lacharite* (charity) for Haiti, as we say in Creole, we refuse. Our answer is no, and we will risk the consequences.

Europe owes us a debt. In fewer than fifteen years, Spain extracted fifteen thousand tons of gold here, after having exterminated the Indians. As for France, we would never finish if we tried to recite all that it took from us. The Pearl of the Antilles supplied the essential basis for its international commerce. Sugar, coffee, and indigo enriched the merchants of Nantes or Rouen while the black people lived like beasts of burden. Once we had acquired our independence, we not only had to dress our wounds, but we were required to pay the old country, which simultaneously quarantined and exploited us. The colonial powers, including the United States, must make amends for the wrong inflicted on the colony or protectorate in those days. The debt experts, when they speak of our liabilities, need to add up the second column of their own accountability.

But we are not beggars. This impoverished land must speak the language of dignity and demand respect, by no means submitting to arrogance or flattery. The historic debt contracted by the nations to the north cannot be paid off by sending us their surplus. I give to the other what is due to him or her, and not what I do not need, what I do not know what to do with.

"Aprè bal tanbou lou" ("After the dance the drums are heavy"). Such a remark coming from the American ambassador, whose humor I appreciate, could in a more distant past have been understood as a warning or as interference: be good children and we will reward you. The full and complete acknowledgment of our legitimacy and of the dignity of the Haitian people ushers in a different interpretation.

The American leadership knew that I was the elected leader of the Haitian people and that I intended to remain faithful to their aspirations as well as to the people's — Caribbean, Latin American and even European — who were taking note of our experience. I could understand the Americans' hesitation. But I was sure that they were ready to cooperate, in the name of a certain tradition and a realistic application of the Monroe Doctrine. We were an alive people who were creating a just state, but who refused charity. On both sides of the Atlantic, people understood this.

I have sometimes been told that the president can no longer use militant language in the face of American imperialism. Governing is not the same thing as staking a claim: the president of all Haitians must necessarily take into account the new parameters that escape the militant fighter. But my historical analysis remains the same. We have passed from total incomprehension to a dialogue marked by respect. The Americans did not cast doubt on the freely expressed will of the Haitian people, and the two sides were drawing nearer to one another. In this way, relations had the potential to flower.

Who would not rejoice to see foreign aid being used in a simple and transparent manner, and no longer diverted by a parasitic state propped up by a bunch of zombie NGOs (associations created for the purpose of turning foreign aid to the profit of the mafia)? Happily, alongside these there were other devoted and efficient organizations that helped the people to survive.

All the international studies confirm that foreign assistance, all of it diverted by the dominant class, had been as wasteful as it was useless. Since 1980, this amounted to two hundred million dollars a year, and these were the same ten years during which the per capita wealth of the country was reduced by 40 percent! In view of that, who would criticize our prudence and our concern that aid should be applied where there was need and controlled by the Haitian authorities who really had authority? The rapacity of those who received often matched the carelessness or ignorance of those who gave.

With the Americans, we had passed from conflict to dialogue. As for the Europeans, many of them were conscious that democracy had been retrieved, and were also aware of the long struggle that had preceded it. "You incarnate the hopes of millions of your compatriots for economic and social justice and for political liberty." I am well aware that diplomatic messages often require decoding, but this one from President Bush after my inauguration contains scarcely any ambiguity. The Haitian tradition of dishonest politics, together with our desire to find trustworthy contacts, made the Americans circumspect. Once a period of transition was past, neither the government nor the business people could have found fault with a regime based on law and honest speaking, even if our dignity made us more sensitive than the cynical, inept and greedy generals of the past.

But our development also had to be built on cooperation with the countries of the south. We have a great deal to offer one another, within a Caribbean sphere that is as diverse as we can make it, together with Latin America and Africa, where our roots are deep. South-south cooperation offers a better approach and a necessary evolution of our relations with the north.

We are all of us involved in the relationship of civilization: if one person suffers somewhere, it matters little where he or she is, for it is all humanity that suffers. If we are concerned to establish a relationship with that person, we do not speak of assistance, but of sharing, of cooperation. The one who suffers has something to bring me, something to teach me. The contribution of the one matches the contribution of the other and excludes any kind of superiority complex. In giving, you receive; in receiving, you give.

As Lahautire, a utopian socialist of the nineteenth century, wrote in his *Petit Catéchisme de la réforme sociale*: "To the extent that anywhere in the whole world there is one single person crying, 'I am hungry, I am cold,' society has not been established." From St. Jean Bosco to the presidential palace, we were pursuing that same utopia, in a restored social fabric, where a person finds happiness in company with other people.

CHAPTER 12

Those Who Eat Once
. . . Sometimes

We had inherited an incredible hierarchy of salaries or incomes: enormous, exaggerated, gigantic, nearly infinite. Imagine, in a country with such weak sources of revenue, a minority leading the same lifestyle as the most favored classes of Europe or North America!

My predecessor, Ertha Pascal Trouillot, enjoyed a salary of ten thousand dollars, plus fifteen thousand for monthly expenses. That does not take into account a good many other advantages that are so well designed to smooth off life's sharp corners. To speak of nothing but salaries, a humble worker in the same palace could earn twenty-four dollars after thirty years of service. And if you push the comparison as far as the mango sellers, as far as the street urchin who cannot get a half dollar a day, you have practically moved from zero to infinity. In what other country can one find distortions like these? That kind of inequality releases in me a feeling of rage mixed with nausea.

It seemed to me, as well as to the ministers, to be a sound move to give an example, showing that we were breaking with the kleptomaniac system that had been in force for decades. Each of us earned about four thousand dollars and had the use of an official car, and that was all. I did not cherish any illusions about the economic impact of such measures, but I thought that a maximum degree of social morality was necessary in order to restore confidence on all sides. Moreover, the cleanup and purification ought to extend all the way to the top.

The lives of some of the ministers and high officials of the old days were on a level with that of a pasha, a viceroy, or a captain of industry. The fee system made it possible for them to double their salaries: fifteen hundred dollars every time they attended a meeting of whatever type. Hooray for gatherings that would give you, in two hours, more than an ordinary Haitian would see in a year! And what was the money for, when the government also furnished servants, cars (including their upkeep), an entertainment allowance, and food? Ah yes, ministers are like all the rest of us: they get hungry sometimes, but never for very long.

As a result of our reforms, there was a shift in the grid of public offices, including those with lower salaries, with the initial negotiations taking place between government, employers and labor unions. The minimum salary of five dollars per working day in major enterprises was the first signal. No one would any longer tolerate a voracious elite who received the whole of the wealth produced by everyone — *"yon lelit ti lolit"* ("a mean and stingy elite").

Redistribution, here as elsewhere, was to be done through fiscal policy. We had no need of new taxes; we simply had to apply the law. In the former system, nobody paid; or, to put it another way, you bought an official or a minister so as not to have to pay taxes. Why should anyone pay taxes? The money only went into the thieves' pockets. The struggle against smuggling and the legitimacy of our government increased the revenues considerably. The transparency of our administration, in addition, enabled anyone to verify the ways in which the money was spent. Smuggling — more than half the products that entered Haiti were smuggled in — and state thievery were going to be severely punished. It was easy to know immediately who was paying a tax, and how much. I relied on the press to provide all the publicity that was necessary.

Nothing was more urgent than a cleanup in every area. Economic efficiency is not compatible with justice, except at the price of a permanent struggle against all the seeds of corruption. That priority of priorities went far beyond the debate over possible hardships or the degree of liberalism that was acceptable for an economy in such a precarious state. People have sometimes ridiculed our economic program or our delays when faced with a system I have described as *restavek*. There can be no doubt that the jargon of the economists or the imperialism of the economy over society (economism), infuriated me as much as the advice and orders coming from outside. It was better to proceed slowly, at our own rhythm, with the insights of those who were in touch with the popular consciousness, than to follow recipes from foreign models provided to us by specialists.

The few large enterprises in the country were often found to be suffering from waste and mismanagement, and from a poor use of their resources; the most profitable had often been the prey or the milk cows of social parasites who had little interest in development or reinvestment. Our move to put them in order did not always make the government highly popular. Stringency is sometimes a long-term investment for those who want to escape from beggary: simplicity and clarity of administration are also good for public enterprises that are too often putrefying as a result of speculation or the squandering of their resources. In reforming themselves, they will be able to benefit from foreign credits which in turn will permit the development of infrastructures that, in our case, were truly lacking: communication networks, energy development, hydraulic projects, and so on.

Competition, whether public or private, does not upset me. In a transformed environment, it may even be desirable. Some new sectors, such as tourism, ought to be developed in that way.

I understand perfectly that investors require a secure climate. They should be reassured that the struggle against Macoutism is a battle for the security of everyone. We were making good progress in that struggle. Haiti was becoming, in every respect, a more secure, a more open, and a more productive country.

But we should not forget that Haiti is not just Port-au-Prince. Three quarters of the population live in the hills. And the best way to prevent the peasants from moving to the city, contributing to a rampant and uncontrolled urbanization, is to discourage them from making a journey from which there can be no return. Certainly the passage of prohibitions or sanctions is no solution: it would be unworkable and contrary to the people's freedom to travel, the freedom of every person. Instead, the solution lies in improving the whole country, creating employment far from the capital city—in short, in making life livable in all parts of Haiti.

Decentralization appeared as a choice that could not be avoided, the antidote to the extension of the urban rubbish heaps. Most migrations ended in failure anyway. Local administration of the problems of schools, sanitation, water, and the creation or maintenance of means of communication were the means to fashion favorable conditions: especially in response to the demands of the peasants which were becoming steadily more strident and forceful.

Land lying fallow, the extreme subdivision of land into "pocket handkerchiefs," property held by a minority: all these were unacceptable. Agrarian reform, written into the Constitution, would not consist of parcelling out the land that was still available. Instead, what we envisaged was a common use and administration, even if only partial, of the tools and the proceeds of labor. There was no single model for this. We were following the wishes of the peasants themselves. The cooperatives we proposed to set up were to be based on the peasants' own social customs and the birth of movements similar to labor unions. There were to be cooperatives for the use of materials, for receiving suggestions, and for improving insufficient yields, and cooperatives for marketing and for the initial processing of primary materials.

The garden cities of which Georges Anglade spoke represented a long-term vision, the result of a marriage between the people and their environment, a slow process that had to be evaluated at each step. Utopia? Not altogether, when one is acquainted with the custom of common work and solidarity. That practice could be deepened, of course, excluding the continued existence of feudal systems of sharecropping and precarious agricultural employment that bound people in servitude. Whether we are talking of peasants or agronomists, we had the human means we needed, and the will to do it.

To transform the peasants into managers, key decision-makers for their living space, was also to guarantee the reconstruction of the natural world. A land that was their very own would be a treasure not to be squandered, but that would reconquer its own self. Planting trees, stopping erosion, preserving ecological balance: all this could thus be an integral part of the new logic.

The ecological tragedy in Haiti is the consequence of anarchy, of economic laissez-faire. In this situation, the peasants could also play the role of an engineering corps for the management of our spaces, whether forest or roads. Our country does not suffer from poor development, as a politics unadapted to its needs might suppose, but from the absence of development, since the governments have never wanted to make any progress in that regard. In the city or in the country, it is necessary to combat anonymity, to return the decisions to those who are most involved. Authority, which has always divided our citizens, should instead encourage them to unite. This was a turn that was easy to announce, but often required delicacy to negotiate.

Moreover, wealth once produced and better distributed would not relieve us of the necessity to solve another basic problem: that of demographic pressure. Ten million Haitians at the dawn of the twenty-first century—is such a thing tolerable? Could we participate in that? Could the country support such a young and numerous population with such a high birthrate? As president and as a theologian, I had a clear answer: no. Let there be no mistake: I had no intention of requiring anyone to practice contraception. Such a constraint would, more than any other, violate the sphere of the most elementary freedoms.

Overpopulation is often the twin of underdevelopment. Increasing levels of education and a rising standard of living are worth more than all the campaigns on behalf of the limitation of births. Each should have the right to choose. Progressively, the feeling will intensify that a large number of children is not necessarily the best way to prepare for the future.

In any case, I reject the idea that, as a priest of the church in Haiti, I should submit to the papal encyclicals that condemn the use of contraception. The gospel is our guide in this case, just as it inspires the bishop of Rome where he is. No one has sole possession of the truth. To encourage individuals to put themselves at risk of conceiving when poverty threatens them is one more form of submission to fate. As a theologian, I am ready to demonstrate that this is false thinking. When Christ said to fill the earth, he did not propose making it overflow! To have reverence for humanity, and even more for women, means to respect their freedom, and even more the freedom of the children yet to come. What is that freedom if there is no milk, if there is no bread for the new arrival? No one can either order or forbid the use of contraceptives. As for the government, which is responsible for the social and demographic situation, its duty should be to explain and to encourage.

To love God is to love the human beings whom I see. My respect for them forbids me to think or decide for them. It is all too easy to make a decision for a woman with no resources while I am swimming in comfort! Contraception is an artificial means? And the prostheses or medicines that stop disease or pain, are we going to condemn those, too? It is a mistaken tactic to hurl anathemas at the use of contraception. Such a condemnation borders on social hypocrisy. The real problem is that of hunger, in a land that could feed all its people, but where the distribution of the land is unjust. The people prostitute themselves or kill to eat or to feed their families. If some people are dreaming of a crusade against the pill or against condoms, I, for my part, am haunted by the hunger that is tormenting so many of the people in my country.

Redistribution, fiscal policy, cleanup, frankness, urbanism, health, schools, communications, ecology, demography, management—which of these was not a priority in a country that had been bled to death, that had suffered so much disaster and had never been rebuilt? What are our priorities?

At this point, I could already speak of some that were in the process of realization. The people were regaining their dignity and their liberty. You could see it all the time in the streets and in the press. Security had made great progress.

But, as we say in Creole, an empty sack cannot stand. There are three kinds of Haitians: a minority who eat whenever they are hungry, a larger number who have one meal a day, and a great many Haitians who eat once . . . sometimes. However patient they may be, these last cannot nourish themselves on nothing but freedom. Freedom loses its meaning when the rich live cheek by jowl with the starving. The opulence displayed by the former cannot go on indefinitely skirting the destitution that afflicts the others. Two years from now, the first of our social measures should enable everyone to eat once a day.

In parallel, a huge task of literacy training had to be undertaken. The goal was to have all the children in school. Finally, the struggle against corruption had to go on without interruption. The appointment of honest and competent officials at every level was an ongoing process in which we were fully engaged.

Today as before, in this task of rebuilding the country, I

remain the shepherd who accompanies his sheep. I am not applying Aristide's program; the popular demands constitute our program as proposed by *Lavalas*. The people's sufferings are my own. I have shared them for so long that there can never be a gap between the president and the aspirations of the majority of Haitians.

In a country where three-quarters of the inhabitants live below the threshold of absolute poverty, we are in search of a Haitian way to happiness. The paradox is only apparent: happiness, though it requires life's minimum, has nothing to do with the unbridled individual consumption of the wealthier nations. "Revolution," as Saint-Just said to a people, the majority of whom were illiterate, "will cease when happiness is perfected."

Let us not forget that, in Haiti, the fibers of our soul vibrate to the rhythm of a country of artists. Music and painting fill the streets and the hills. These people who have never been able to go to school have spontaneously entered into the school of the arts. That instruction is omnipresent, free, and open to all types of feelings. Look at the decorated *taptap* (small buses), which convey as much of the national identity as does the popular struggle. The artistic dimension has preserved us from the worst. Without that lifting of our thoughts in which everyone can participate, we would more easily have sunk into final despair or nihilism. The painting that is called naive has enabled us to retain our hope intact.

We have lost two centuries, but I see myself primarily as a child of the people engaged in a revolutionary struggle for legality. The Haitians have been ready for democracy for a long time, but their leaders have, until now, devoted the heart of their energies to keeping the future at bay. What remains for me to do—and very quickly, all of it—is important, and it troubles me more than the new hat I am wearing.

When the poorest people say: "Titid is the little me," their affection touches me as much as their trust and their nearness. Together, we have come through the dangers, and it is our expectation to go beyond hope.

CHAPTER 13

Murdered Hope

After two centuries in search of democracy, and eight months in an attempt that was completely new in our history, hope was about to waver once more. Would the intrusion of brutal power again block a people's march toward its promised land? For the military caste and a handful of the privileged, the people's recovery of their dignity and the laying of the keel of the first reforms were too much.

Persistent rumors of a military coup d'état were poisoning the atmosphere at the end of September, when I returned from New York. I had just been at the General Assembly of the United Nations to measure the undeniable international support for the new Haiti (see Chapter 16). The military barracks had already given us some concern. In the spring, the soldiers had risen against their officers.

There were two particular cases: the mutinies in Pétion-ville and in the navy. In the first instance, I had gone to see the soldiers who had revolted against a captain whom they accused of continued despotic behavior. In spite of many people's advice, I went into the barracks myself. The soldiers obeyed me: against the tenor of their resolutions, they agreed to salute the officer whose window they had just shot to pieces. I had listened to the lower ranks, while avoiding the humiliation of a hierarchical superior. He was, after all, only one cog in the repressive machine. He was playing his part as he had been taught to do.

The sailors' demands were also legitimate. I gave satisfaction to the rank and file, while explaining to them that the violence and contempt from which they suffered were the results of a system that we were all battling together. That seems to be the way in which a government responsible to all the people ought to operate.

On the evening of Sunday, September 29, shots were heard at the Frères camp, a few kilometers from Port-au-Prince. This time the rumor of mutiny was transformed into the noise of automatic weapons. The director of the national radio, Michel Favard, a brave man, also announced that a coup d'état was imminent. He would be kidnapped immediately afterward by a military commando troop. Before they were cut off, the radio stations had called for vigilance against the suspicious movements of part of the army.

On the previous evening, I had called General Cédras to ask his feeling about the rumors, to which I still gave little credence. He supported me in my skepticism, and we laughed about it together. How can I help feeling some remorse now, when I think of the thousands of dead and remember the tranquil calm I then felt, which at that time seemed to be so completely justified?

Cédras, whom I had appointed head of the general staff on February 7, 1991, and later commander-in-chief of the army, had taken part in the organization of the elections in December 1990. He was a young officer of the new generation, commissioned in 1971, from a class born under Jean-Claude Duvalier. I had chosen to cultivate a good deal of confidence in our relationship. There was very little suspicion: he had often remarked on his attachment to the democratic process.

On Sunday I received the same reassuring response from Cédras, but by evening there could be no more doubt about the rebellion: my house was surrounded and bullets were spattering against its walls again. Friends and militants who were already there or who came in great numbers were massacred. Before the demonstrators could assemble or barricades be erected, the military emptied their magazines at everything that moved. They had learned the lesson of Lafontant's coup d'état: at all costs, they had to prevent the people from gathering, barricades from being erected, and a popular insurrection from being unleashed. Assisted by Macoute bands apparently coming from the Dominican Republic, they sowed death everywhere. The corpses were counted in the tens and hundreds. The terror was carried out in the most brutal form in order to discourage any popular reaction. *Lafanmi Selavi* was a target once again, along with the populous neighborhoods (Cité-Soleil, Carrefour), where the people attempted with the most pitiful means to provide some opposition to the soldiery. The young partisans of *Lavalas* paid a heavy price.

The night was shattered by cries and by the incessant noise of automatic weapons. It was impossible for me to leave my house, which had been transformed into a bunker. It was equally impossible for me to send out an appeal that would be heard. The radio transmitters had been occupied or destroyed by the military, and the airwaves were hopelessly mute. I owe the fact that I emerged alive from my house to a few diplomats, especially the French ambassador, Jean-Raphael Dufour, who took the risk of coming to get me. A convoy was moving toward the presidential palace. One of our soldiers was killed. Along the route, we were attacked several times.

Had the whole army risen, or was this a mutiny by a few isolated units, supported by the Macoute leaders like Franck Romain or William Régala? As soon as we reached the National Palace, I called Cédras to get to the bottom of things.

It is a trick! The building is surrounded! I have only a few reliable friends with me. I try to leave with the others, to avoid a civil war. My object is to talk with them, to negotiate, perhaps to persuade them. Guns are crackling outside. One of those beside me falls dead. I have already experienced similar situations: I throw myself to the ground. Death is prowling closer. I have just obtained a new respite: but for how long?

One of our heroes, Captain Fritz Pierre-Louis, has been killed in cold blood. It is incredible, but true; a crime, a horror. At the same time I feel, I know that my friends, my brothers and sisters who live crowded together in the lower city are under fire. We leave the palace as prisoners, headed for the army general headquarters. Cédras is there; he hid his cards very well. Smart and sprightly in the uniform of his high rank, he is smiling, calm, even cheerful and condescending. He tells me plainly, with a glowing countenance: "From now on, I am the president." Eight of my companions are tortured and beaten by the soldiers.

Cédras is pleased with himself. The officers drink to his health. There is the atmosphere of a macabre festival alongside the bloodied faces of my friends. I myself have my hands tied. They try to humiliate me. The military discuss my fate in loud tones. "We ought to kill him." They almost get into an argument about who will have the pleasure of doing it. International reaction—France? the United States?—is worrisome to the more "political" among them. They hesitate. They deliberate, haggling over lives, mine in particular. The pressure applied by the democratic countries wins the day: I will leave, finally, on the plane sent by Carlos Andrés Pérez, the president of Venezuela, a friend whose tenacity is irresistible.

Exhausted by forty-eight hours of sleeplessness and extreme tension, my face distorted with sorrow for my many friends, whether close or unknown, I spoke only one phrase into the Venezuelan night: "mission accomplished, my conscience is at peace." I would not bargain away universal approbation as Cédras had negotiated for our heads, after having caused the death of so many others.

Why, after we had tried so hard to reconcile it with the people, did the machinery of death set itself in motion again, still more savagely than under Namphy or Avril? It was because we had determined to pursue reform of the army; to separate the army from the police, as the Constitution demands; to divert the institution from its taste for politics and its claim to be allowed to intervene whenever its interests were threatened—interests that some people often confused with dividends, special revenues, secret receipts or rackets. The proceeds of corruption, smuggling, and still more of drug traffic were diminishing. There was no question of abating our determination to put a stop to those practices. Nor was there any question of renouncing our intention to bring the army into its proper role in a government of laws. The Constitution demanded it, and besides, the Haitians had elected me for that purpose. There was no other reason for the coup d'état. The people of privilege, not all of them belonging to the army, slaughtered hundreds of innocents—the mob, as they said—to preserve their prerogatives and extend their own dealings.

And sure enough, two days later, in the face of an aroused international opinion, Cédras and his friends tried to furnish some less "corporative" explanations. The apparent cynicism of the move was far from their thoughts: they had acted out of altruism, out of respect for the Haitian people, for democracy, and so on. Cédras the Just had sacrificed himself to unmask Aristide the Dictator—and to denounce the ongoing violations of the Constitution and of civil justice, and the flouting of human rights.

There was not a single prisoner of conscience in the Haitian prisons. When one has been looking for it for such a long time, the road of democracy is sometimes difficult to follow. The death of an honest politician like Sylvio Claude is unacceptable. But who profited from the crime, or from the provocation? Moreover, Haiti had never known such a democratic and peaceful ferment as during those eight months. In fact, the accusations of a felonious general, the organizer of a campaign of terror that cost a thousand lives, did not deserve any response. He would confiscate democracy in order to better establish liberty!

Cédras is no more nor less savage, felonious and greedy
for power than his predecessors, the Duvaliers, Lafontant,
Namphy, or Avril. His temperament is as macabre and vile
as theirs: he promises "respect for the Constitution and elections"—free ones, I suppose? We are even told that he is a
moderate. A moderate torturer? Still far from the records
set by the Duvaliers? Namphy and Avril were ordinarily "satisfied" with oppression in three figures, but with Cédras we
have already reached four digits!

Never since the time of François Duvalier had such a
slaughter been seen: hundreds of victims during the night
hours of September 29-30, daily machine-gunning of the
slums during the curfew, forcing the inhabitants to an urban
exodus, families forced *manu militari* to dig in the cemeteries
to bury their own dead, whole truckloads of corpses, the
sadism of the new chief of police, Michel François. If we were
to carry out an exhaustive inventory, it would be a long one,
as long as the oppression carried out against those whom the
sinister leader of this band referred to on January 23, 1992,
as "the unnaturals"—a notion that recalls the worst totalitarian regimes.

After the military coup—"a corrective operation"—came
the constitutional coup. Cédras quickly realized that his
power was illegitimate, unacceptable, and intolerable, within
the country and outside. He shouted loud and long that he
had not acted on behalf of the army, and that he would step
aside for a provisional president. With Aristide considered
as having resigned, and Préval refusing to emerge from hiding
(to be executed?), the machine-gunners turned their aim on
the members of parliament and forced them to appoint Nér-
ette, a poor puppet pulled from the dictator's pocket.

Cédras was a political magician. He benefited from the
cowardice of part of the political class who were less fearless
than the social forces that continued to resist. The political
leaders clearly condemned the *pronunciamento* of October 1;

the government named a week later was already exciting the jealousy and the appetites of some people. Let there be no mistake: I am not referring to the people who assented under unbearable pressure. As we say here, "the Constitution is made of paper, but the bayonets are made of steel." But no one in such circumstances is forced to be enthusiastic or to offer loyal cooperation. How could anyone extend a hand to those who were standing on top of a mountain of corpses, their feet bathed in the blood of the victims and their arms open to receive the assassins? How could anyone tolerate the appointment to positions of command of individuals convicted of corruption, extortion, influence peddling and already caught with their hands in the till?

That a former candidate for the presidency energetically condemned the putsch and its consequences: that is something praiseworthy in an avowed democrat. When the same man announces eight days later, in the name of his movement, "a technical helping hand for the provisional government," he returns us to the old demons of Haitian politics. There are always would-be democrats who are ready to extend a helping hand to the coup organizers. Among the dozens of existing parties, their membership sometimes limited to a single family, one can easily find a few collaborators eager to grasp the opportunity of their political lives and to take the suddenly shortened route that leads to power—or the appearance of power.

With the exception of the dens of Macoutes, avowed or disguised, I respect all the political parties, their advice, and their proposals. Fidelity to popular aspirations is one of the criteria for my judgment. Their attitude in face of a coup constitutes an excellent revealer of the behavior of each of them.

Please, let us make an end of this political pathology that transforms dozens of leaders—each the head of a microscopic unit—into so many presidential candidates, some of them free, to speed up the rhythm of presidential elections in order to seize their own opportunities. Let us get away from this childishness. On February 8, 1991, I had chosen a government representative from those two Haitians out of three who voted for *Lavalas*. In light of the consequences of the tragic military adventure, and an economy, in particular, that is more lifeless than it was a year ago, unity is indispensable. Our economy, ruined by decades of robbery, is about to lose hundreds of millions of dollars from foreign sources. Commerce has dried up; production is reduced; the currency is weakened; the beginnings of confidence have dissolved. The Haitian people are being forced to flee as evidenced by the exodus from the urban centers and the flight of the boat people. The economy has been reduced to organized theft and a traffic in drugs whose extraordinary expansion has been attested by observers. At the brink of the abyss, we must gather all our energies together.

The old democracies were built slowly. The prescriptions of the recent or more distant past can be studied, tried, amended. I certainly made mistakes, as did others. Condemnations or accusations of guilt can only lead to speedier decomposition. More important is the minimum—or the maximum—that democrats have in common. To speed up the reforms, to expand the sphere of democracy, to do justice, to improve the quality of the government: all these things are possible, on condition that debate and participation are not the prerogatives of the privileged classes; on condition that sharing and social urgency take precedence over the political game or race. Politics cannot be conducted without mutual respect between the legislature and the executive. Democracy is defended and built up every day, and we all have a great deal to learn before we can put it into practice.

It is also necessary that we rebuild the army and the police: a task as overwhelming as it will be to overcome the divorce between them and the people. The leading groups who are guilty of crimes against humanity, must be brought to justice.

A great many soldiers who have been abused and brain-washed were panicked by a fear of unemployment or of the disintegration of their institution. Others were afraid or found no other solution but to obey. Some deserted, and some officers were demoted or dismissed by the general staff. The people have always been victimized by the army. In the name of love, because I have been faithful to the cause of nonviolence for twenty years, I have opposed the law of retaliation. I have acted and I will act to create a commission of inquiry to restore and purify the army; the commission will determine responsibility without judging the army collectively. The victims know me. We will have to create the means for this change: those who drive the tanks and those with empty stomachs who cry out their need for dignity should know they are part of the same family. Even if I should lose some support, the poor should not be punished or forgotten.

The international community can play a deciding role in the reconquest of democracy. The putsch-makers have grossly underestimated the importance and the legitimacy conferred by universal suffrage, as well as the effects of blind massacres, the futility of their pseudo-constitutional disguise, the power of nonviolence, and the unanimity of those in exile. The political isolation of the usurpers and the international condemnation of the spectacle of hope put to the sword impose new duties on us: to be worthy of the support we have received, and to eliminate barbarism down to its roots. To govern Haiti means, in the eyes of observers, to accept a wager, to be suicidal, or to be an exorcist. Every upheaval makes the task more difficult.

Do we have any other choice, *"tèt ansanm"* ("all together"), than to take up the challenge? We are forced to it, but with hope, a nourishment of which we have an enormous store, and the assurance that the most beautiful things are, ultimately, the most difficult to accomplish. But the Haitian people love beauty so very much.

CHAPTER 14

Epilogue: Stronger Than the Gun[*]

Months after the coup d'état of September 30, 1991, in Haiti, we are still seeking the solution to our crisis. This is both a cruel joke and a tragedy.

It is a tragedy because more than 2,000 people have been killed, while about 20,000 more have gone into exile, fleeing the repression. Thousands of others are in hiding. There exists no freedom of the press nor other civic freedoms.

This is also a tragedy because the people of Haiti want democracy. They have already had seven months of democracy, and they do not want to go back to dictatorship. Since the coup, they have been fighting for the restoration of democracy, but have been unable to attain it.

Herein is the cruel joke. The resolution of the crisis—re-establishment of democracy—is obvious, in spite of the contradictions of the negotiations process.

This is because the visible, operable power right now is based on weapons, and those weapons are in the hands of

[*]The information contained in this Epilogue was originally published in an article in *Sojourners* (July 1992). It was written by Jean-Bertrand Aristide in collaboration with Beverly Bell, formerly a coordinator of the Haiti Communications Project. Used with permission of *Soujourners*, Box 29272, Washington, D.C. 20017 (202-636-3637).

General Raoul Cédras, the ringleader of the coup, and his gang of thugs. Behind the de facto government (which the military placed in power after overthrowing my administration) is this real power: the gun. Through their military equipment, Cédras and his gang of soldiers are imposing their will.

Those who are not very familiar with Haiti may think that the de facto, illegitimate government represents the current dominant power. This misperception has been fostered by those who want to support Cédras and his gang, and who have hidden behind the de facto government to do so. The Haitian Parliament is also being used as a smoke screen for what is really going on, as is a delegation from Parliament that has participated in the Organization of American States-sponsored negotiations. Some members of the international community, of course, understand quite well who the invisible actors are.

We who are fighting for democracy have another power: theological power. We have resistance, which is rooted in theology. This is based in Haitians' belief in justice, which for us is God. Our faith in the light provided by liberation theology makes our own reality clear to us.

We are not looking for a God living off in the distance. God, in our minds, has taken the close and immediate form of justice; Jesus was the king of justice. For the Haitian people, fighting for justice means following the direction of our faith. And they are consistent in the way they understand God and the way they are seeking to attain God/justice.

From this foundation of faith, the people have clearly stated no to numerous situations that were not fostering justice. For instance, on December 16, 1990, the citizens of Haiti expressed their will through the ballot. Justice asks that they be granted the results of what they demanded and earned on that day. But this has not been the case. Since the coup d'état of September 30, 1991, the people continue to try to attain the results of that vote, and to attain a just life.

This faith and determination of the Haitian people represents a theological power. In spite of the army's weapons,

Haitians continue to build, and by so doing demonstrate that they are not afraid of the paralysis of the gun. That allows the Haitian people to transcend to a movement where spiritual power is stronger than the power of the gun. The faith and communion involved are obvious to those who can see beyond the naked eye.

Another strength of theological power lies in its basis in community, which goes far beyond individuals or a single people. We see in the Bible the community's ability to share life and thereby make life better; and we see the same reality in Haiti, where the community is trying to improve life, to change the current situation so as to give a direction to history.

Jesus did that in his life. Common people met with Jesus in the practice of community. This was not just a community in theory, but in practice; people were actively living that which was in their blood, in their minds, in their hearts.

Though there are 2,000 years separating us, the Haitian community today follows the same movement, the same communion, as Jesus' community. We saw death in Jesus' time, too. Then, they killed people who thirsted for justice. They do the same in Haiti today. "They" refers to those who control the political keys without knowing how strong the theological keys are.

THE POWER OF LOVE

Let us compare political power with theological power. On the one hand, we see those in control using the traditional tools of politics: weapons, money, dictatorship, coups d'état, repression. On the other hand, we see tools that were used 2,000 years ago: solidarity, resistance, courage, determination, and the fight for dignity and might, respect and power. We see transcendence. We see faith in God, who is justice.

The question we ask now is this: which is stronger, political power or theological power? I am confident that the latter is stronger. I am also confident that the two forces can converge, and that their convergence will make the critical difference.

That convergence is predicated on the power of love. This is the capacity to realize that each of us is part of the other. If we can deeply empathize with the way another feels, we become stronger. This capacity empowers us to defy patterned responses and automatic reflexes.

Suppose that we come to possess military weaponry, the same weaponry our predecessors had. Tradition tells us to shoot the way they shot, to kill the way they killed. What stops us is this capacity to feel how bad we ourselves would feel—indeed, have felt—under the rifle barrel. Our identification and empathy provide us the power not to obey the traditional voice to hurt others.

We call that love. If we do not love others, it is almost impossible to ascribe another's feelings to ourselves. This love is neither an intellectual concept nor a sentimental feeling. It is a force that one gains because one is open to it, because one has the seeds in one's blood—which may have been implanted through education or culture. The more the seeds develop inside one, the more one will be able to feel the way another feels.

This inevitably brings us far from the field of traditional politics, which is narrow and oppressive. One need only look at the world, with its structures of repression and corruption, to realize that. In contrast, the power of love is freeing, allowing us not to simply replicate tradition. We are not machines, and we have the vision and options available to us to rise above and beyond in the power of love. The challenge and the key is to be in connection with others, not just ourselves, in which way we become free.

This gives us the theological key. Because God is love, and living things possess a form of power, we are already living in God's power. No matter what name one gives to God, if one believes God is love and attempts to act from God's power, one has discovered God. This is why theology is critical to the crisis in which the people of Haiti are living. The roots of the world come from God's words.

God is love and justice. You cannot know love and stray far from justice. And you cannot move to justice and go far from love. The two words express the same reality. Not everyone can understand this because some people have rejected the idea of God from the start.

POLITICAL POWER

Our current political situation is a result of a long course of traditional politics, based on the goal of winning. The rules are rigid: The more power an individual or institution amasses from money or weapons, the greater the chance of winning; strength comes from an ability to impose one's will on others; dishonesty is immaterial relative to the goal; killing human beings is immaterial; dictatorship is immaterial; victory is paramount. This is the way we usually understand politics (even though those with the weaponry and capital sometimes say that politics is promoting the welfare of the community).

Those in Haiti who perpetrated the coup d'état felt they had won at first, because they were able to impose their will and break the trajectory of the democratic process. Finally they have been forced to realize that the community's own goals have held steadfast, and that they have not attained victory.

While ethics is not a strong component of the army and those supporting the coup, we still realize the difference between their ethics and ours. Their ethics is based on winning the game through the free reign of weapons and money. As for us, we say, "Regardless of the strength of your economic might or your military hardware, you will never be the victor."

We do not count up the ante or check the board to determine if we are winning or losing. For here is our ethic: we feel we are the victors when there are no losers. We feel that way because we share each other's reality. If we were to use weapons or money to impose our point of view, those who have set themselves out as our opponents would become the losers. Because we share their reality, we, too, would be defeated. And since that is not our goal, neither do we want them to lose.

Our stance pushes us in a direction where there are neither winners nor losers. We seek a reality where together we can triumph. We call this the ethic of love, because love is doing for others what you want people to do for you. This ethic allows us to explore a new world, to build a new society. The rules of this society are not the same as the old world, which requires tools of domination for victory. The new world works to transform a generation of losers into a generation of winners, in which people will realize the beauty of working together.

This is the kind of politics we want in Haiti. It is not the realpolitik that dictates the affairs of most of the world. This one will provide a much more positive result. For instance, in realpolitik people have been talking about justice, freedom, and democracy for thousands of years. But what, in fact, has developed in the world?

In Haiti, for instance, we still have an illiteracy rate of 85 percent. We still have about 4,000 families — that is, about 1 percent of the population — who control more than 45 percent of the nation's wealth and resources. Those who today control the political and economic structures in Haiti are still talking about justice, democracy, and freedom. The question we ask those who have placed our country in its current state is, "When you talk about these concepts, are you loving people? Do you empathize with — or even care about — their suffering? And if you have no sense of the way they feel, how can you change the structures of exploitation to make people's lives more fulfilled?"

THE POWER TO CHANGE

Traditional politics always concerns a competition of forces, in which the stronger force is the winner. And these forces are protected by wealth, arms, and certain institutions. How can we prevail over the strong and their instruments of domination?

I believe only the force of love can push people to stop using weaponry and economic power to maintain the current reality of grinding poverty, vastly unequal distribution of resources, repression, and violent rule. Once people start to realize that they love others, they will start to change the way they use their means of power in politics. Once those who have the structures of weapons and money in their hands become motivated by love, they will yield to the necessity of changing oppressive structures.

If, on the other hand, those who control economic and military power feel that those who are victims of their structures — that is, the poor — hate them, they will have no interest in changing the conditions of life for the poor, or in collaborating with them. If those who have the tools of domination in their hands can intellectually understand the reactions of the poor — that anger is a normal psychological reaction to oppression — we can transcend a war between people. We can perceive the existent structures as nothing more than a mechanism of traditional society, and decide to go forward from there to create a new paradigm of politics.

We cannot wait for change, because change will never come on its own. Instead, acting from liberation theology, from love, and from our spirit of resistance, we must ask and fight for change. We do not need to succumb to hatred or revenge in so doing; the issue at hand is simply one of justice. We must use politics as a strategy to reject the current reality of misery and exploitation.

At the same time, we say yes to those who control weapons and money, because we want them to be part of our process of change. We know how hard the necessary changes may be for them, but we are leaving the door open to speak to them face to face, and to share our point of view with them. We are seeking to build a new bridge, leading to a new kind of politics. If the rich are afraid to come to this bridge and listen to the poor, then the poor will continue to go to that bridge.

We have confidence that this transformation of politics, through a new definition and application of power, can occur. We have seen the beginnings in Haiti. Though the process was truncated by those unwilling to accept the vision of convergence of theological and political power, those who are living in God/justice refuse to give up. Because traditional political paradigms fail too miserably, we must continue our experiment of living in the power of love.

III

Convictions

CHAPTER 15

My Convictions

Perhaps, in place of racism as it exists in America, Haiti has a terrible case of contempt on the part of one social category for the other?

This phenomenon certainly exists. The dirty politicians (and I use that expression deliberately) have, in the past, often set the blacks against the mulattos, making use of the difference in color. Parallel to that, the favored groups in society are often prepared to defend their advantages by any means necessary: hence the contempt of some for the misfortunes of others. We have more social segregation than racism in its pure form. However, at present the *Lavalas* movement is uniting the people with one part of the bourgeoisie. For the latter, the road to unity, the desire for national reconstruction are more powerful than class interests.

We are sometimes close to a caste system, or to a system in which superiority complexes are expressed quite crudely...

Individual behavior is often related to family reputation in the broad sense. There is, effectively, a group of families — the court — who have an ingrained sense of superiority and regard others as beasts of burden, as nonentities, and then there is a majority of Haitians who live a form of socialism related to their own roots, going back to an era in which that word did not even exist. For them, solidarity is stronger than their differences.

Does the candidate of the poor consider himself a poor man?

I was not born into a rich family, and I never had occasion to work for the purpose of accumulating money. I have always lived among the dispossessed. It is true that circumstances have given me economic, and especially cultural, resources that are inaccessible to them. I may consider myself to be a privileged poor man living in the midst of the poor.

Is there a limit to the patience of the poor?

Deceived and humiliated as they have been, they could well have lost all confidence in political action. They have had time to measure the degree of contrast. Their patience was related to certain objectives: work, food, respect, justice, dignity. They saw what was going on, assessed their impediments and their strengths. But the mere fact that someone was talking about them, that someone was grounding political action on the elementary needs of the greater number, appeared incongruous or intolerable to a tiny but influential minority, a group of the wealthy who cannot bear that *tout moun se moun*. For them, the border between "the literate" and "the bums" is to remain impermeable, a fortress bristling with watchtowers. When it confronts this wall of contempt, a patience that loses hope turns to rage.

Are you not presuming that people are more idealistic than they really are?

Haitians have always fought for freedom, whether the oppressor is a colonialist or another Haitian. Today, they are doing nothing more than persevering in their choice and continuing their history. We prefer to die standing up rather than to live as beggars or give up. If the process that is now going on has only one objective, it is to make any return to slavery impossible, whether it is the slavery of the body or that of the mind.

Martinique and Guadeloupe, which remained French possessions, have a per capita income twenty times that of Haiti. It may be that the average mango-seller would rather live there . . .

How many future Haitians, when they were being transported from Africa, threw themselves into the sea? How many Haitians today choose to live here in order to live better tomorrow? I would wager that they would be an overwhelming majority. When they become boat people, uprooted, exploitable at anyone's will, or when they become cane cutters in Santo Domingo, they quickly change their tune. Paradise is not something you can go in search of. The illusion of freedom is right under their noses. Yesterday, too, they would have preferred to return, but they could not.

What would you say to all the people you see embarking as boat people headed for Florida?

I would not harangue them. I would try to translate my thoughts into action, into sharing. What can we do together to satisfy our hunger, to resolve the economic problems that are driving them from the country? I would tell them that we can struggle today in Haiti instead of dying at sea; that the land of Haiti is willing to give them the place they deserve; that underdevelopment is not fatal.

But when the mercenaries are spreading terror every moment, what can one say to them? Before the putsch, you know, the exodus had dried up. Suffering was still there, but everyone chose to remain. With the return of the Haitian boat people intercepted by the U.S. ships, the high point of hypocrisy, arbitrariness, and racism has been reached. Protests are multiplying, but what difference do they make?

How can we view this exodus—like the one that is emptying the slums that are too exposed to police brutality—

except as a consequence of the coup d'état? It is the moral wretchedness on which terrorism is based; it is political repression that forces hundreds of thousands of Haitians to flee or to hide. Does anyone want to blame them for the oppression that has fallen upon them? Will they continue to be sent back? Who is being protected, the executioners or the victims?

The independence of Haiti—the first in that region—was betrayed by a checkmate. It was premature; the country was cruelly short of trained people . . .

No. The maturity existed, and the ability as well. But the enemy destroyed everything before isolating the country completely, placing us in an impossible situation. Fear of contagion rendered the colonialists savage; they thought that the whole Caribbean might be affected by that bad example.

You are sometimes criticized for your lack of interest in general economics. Frankly, you don't care much for that discipline, do you?

I certainly prefer the humanities, those fields that make the human being the focus of their research. Economic liberalism, which demagogues and technocrats have made a panacea, I find intolerable. The economists' superiority complex, and their propensity to try to control everything, is unacceptable.

However, in the course of acquiring various degrees, I did study economics. I am passionately fond of that discipline when it is placed at the service of human beings, when it takes their practices and their know-how into account. Having said all that, I am all too well aware of the importance of economics, and I am sufficiently conscious of my deficiencies to ask for advice or to place confidence in economists—provided they never forget that the object of every action is the human being.

"The rich are not supposed to give orders to the poor," you have said. What did you mean by that?

Wealth, financial superiority, and arrogance all end in making one certain that one possesses the truth, and they generally predispose people to use repression or to compromise with dictatorial regimes. The wealthy have often become what they are by virtue of exploiting others. The fact that that analysis goes back to the nineteenth century does not make it outmoded. We are living on top of a permanent and ongoing extortion directed at the most impoverished.

Above all, the international rules are made to prevent those who are under the table from some day taking their place at the common feast. They can be made to wait for centuries. They need to shake the table, even to overturn it — with all the risks that that action implies.

Is it possible to cooperate with the North without accepting the liberal system?

Yes. "Marronage," the life of the runaways, was one of our responses to the colonial system. The runaway slaves, the "maroons," fleeing from the plantations, shifted for themselves, creating their own economic system. Again today we have a kind of scientific "marronage" uniting tactics and technology. But we are not naive; we are open to all investments and all kinds of cooperation, provided that they respect us as we are.

But international criteria treat Haitian peasants lightly.

They were making fun of us up to the day of December 16, 1990. Then came the surprise of my election, and especially the triumph of *Lavalas*. The same surprise is awaiting them on the economic plane. It will be a pleasant surprise, since the Haitian peasants are beginning to organize themselves. Their willingness, supported by agrarian reform, should enable the country to become self-sufficient in its food supply, especially rice.

Could you profit from Franco-American rivalry?

Two powers are seeking to preserve their interests in a diplomatic context, each from its own point of view. Both of them are present in the Caribbean. The French have a cultural advantage related to our roots and our linguistic ties. On the American side, the economic and strategic interests are obvious. Certainly, Haiti is not for sale. I am prepared to accept cooperation from both sides.

1492–1992: the world is celebrating the quincentenary of the discovery of America. When you hear the name of Christopher Columbus, how do you react?

I see a big white man, a colonial; the man who, by "discovering" America, stole it from those who were living there and exploited it. His successors, the conquistadors, revealed "Quesqueya"—the Indian name of the island before its "discovery"—to our ancestors. What comes to my mind when I think of Christopher Columbus is the mutilation of many peoples and the beginning of a long chain of injustices.

His statue in Port-au-Prince has been pulled down and thrown into the sea. That was one expression of the rage of a victimized group. The cross he carried in his hand had nothing to do with ours. His was a cross of slavery, and ours proclaims liberation. But Christopher Columbus was only the first. The conquistadors, the French colonials of the eighteenth century or the American occupiers at the beginning of the twentieth, yielded nothing at all to him in the realm of contempt and brutality.

The year 1992 marks five hundred years of robbery and five hundred years of resistance. We can celebrate the resistance, but we certainly cannot express any joy at having been "discovered."

With rather rare exceptions, churchmen have encouraged colonialism.

The Catholic church cooperated totally with slavery and exploitation, without hesitation and without remorse. The priests were the real colonialists. Their guilt and complicity extends into the twentieth century. In the struggle for the second independence, everyone had to take sides: for resignation or for resistance.

The church suffers because of its past. It is uneasy with history. It needs to look at it as it was, no matter how painful the examination of conscience may be.

Before your election, you named the enemies of the Haitian people: the army allied with the Macoutes, the oligarchy and its politicians, the United States, the Catholic hierarchy. Has that gang of four been re-established?

Listen to the cries of seven million Haitians, those inside the country and those outside who can express themselves more freely. The tumult of their revolt pointed out those responsible. Certainly not everyone has the same degree of guilt, but all of them stand accused.

It took the Pope 65 days to condemn the oppression . . .

Does that surprise you? For those who know the Pope and the majority of the Haitian bishops, it was no surprise. It would be the reverse that would produce astonishment. In the long struggle against the post-Duvalier dictatorships, we always found the Catholic hierarchy barring the way to emancipation. Their rallying to me after my inauguration was nothing but opportunism. I think that the Vatican should stand in the front rank among those countries that have made every effort to retard our return to democratic processes. While so many nations are reducing their diplomatic representation in Haiti, the Vatican has just named a new nuncio!

Two thousand dead, twenty thousand political refugees, two hundred thousand people who are fugitives in their own country: that is more than any of the peoples of Eastern Europe have paid for their emancipation. Over there, the Vatican did not wait two months to react! We are deeply saddened by the thought that they are settling accounts with the theology of liberation to the neglect of one of the most impoverished and courageous peoples on earth.

Do you think that collusion between the dictatorship and the Catholic hierarchy has been proved?

It is simply obvious. What we have here is a battle of the hierarchy against the people, dictated by higher authorities, a veritable demonstration against the gospel. Quite obviously, the bishops do not use the same vocabulary as the putsch-makers. But they give credence to the idea that there has never been democracy in Haiti. Hierarchy-oligarchy-army: we know the orchestra by heart, even if each of them plays a different instrument. There is a genuine complementarity, in the tradition of the aborted coup of January 1991, in which the archbishop of Port-au-Prince played a duet with Roger Lafontant, the head of the Tontons Macoute.

Are the great majority of priests who denounced the attacks on elementary freedoms protected by their hierarchy?

Bishop Romélus of Jérémie, who condemned the putsch, is the object of ongoing persecution. His assistants have been arrested and are effectively hostages; the bishop himself is continually threatened.

How could one say that those who are ignoring this colleague of theirs are demonstrating anything but a complicitous silence in face of the persecutions of those priests who continue to speak out, and those people who are resisting? The statement issued by the episcopal conference at the O.A.S. testifies to its support of the coup d'état, not to any solidarity with the Haitian clergy.

If a distinction is made between power and authority, could one say that the people are the power and you are the authority?

That question is both amusing and relevant. I used those two words to describe the governments that followed one another from 1986 to 1990: they had power, but they lacked authority. One of them, that of Manigat, had neither.

The military governments combined all sorts of power: weapons, the police, and money because they were favored by the oligarchy. Take away Cédras's tanks, and he is naked. Authority can only be bestowed by the Haitians, all the Haitians. As the French revolutionaries proclaimed, the people are sovereign. The military, completely devoid of authority, can only govern through fear.

But I freely acknowledge that power should be in the hands of the people. I would have the authority, on condition that the two things go hand in hand. I cannot detach myself from the people: our relationship is a marriage, a communion, a fusion, in which each plays his or her own part so that all can hear the political symphony better.

Is it possible to resist Titid? Are there disagreements, for example, in the government, about concrete problems?

That has already happened, and, frankly, I did not suffer because of it. On the contrary, such an attitude helps me, as before, to understand better, to make corrections, to make things complete. My limits are those of any human being: I do not possess intuitive knowledge, and I have serious gaps here and there. And yet I am perhaps a bit of a psychologist: no one should ever pretend to know everything.

In the Council of Ministers, we used to take votes, and it sometimes happened that Titid was in the minority. Naturally, I gave way. I have no desire at all to work with a lot of flatterers.

Do you consider the president's job to be a kind of political priesthood?

It really is a priesthood. Like the pastor, I accompany the sheep. I share the people's sufferings. Their claims are mine. I constantly keep in mind the needs and the demands of the dispossessed.

Do you like the expression "priest-president" that the journalists use?

They are not lying: I am priest and president. But I remain what I have always been, even if my office demands some compromises: I am a militant in the midst of a people who want to emerge from the shadows.

And if there is talk of a prophet-president?

Why not? Anyone who assumes his or her responsibilities, who is not afraid to say what she or he sees, can be regarded as a prophet, or, better, as the spokesperson of a prophetic community.

I am inclined to see in you a certain resemblance to Robespierre.

There is no question that there are common denominators between us and the makers of the French Revolution: 1789 is an essential reference point, as is 1793. The memory of the heroes of the rights of humanity should always be in our minds, as their texts are in our hands. Robespierre himself denounced the "patripockets." From Saint-Just to Abbé Grégoire, how much I owe to the makers of the Revolution! Most of them had a global vision of human liberation.

Obviously, the Salesians approached the French Revolution with diplomacy and reserve. They wanted to rescue the stakes of the church, which had mistakenly chosen the wrong side.

Robespierre was called "the incorruptible."

That is a rare quality in politics, and it doesn't always make for a long term in office.

One question that you yourself have brought up: could you last long? Are you not at the mercy of a new assassination attempt?

I do not always have a choice. The military wanted to kill me on September 30, 1991, and no doubt others will try it.

I often think about it. No one in this world is indispensable. But I am glad to remain what I am and where I am. I would be very happy to fill out all five years of my term. The work to be done is so exciting that I would be glad if fate permitted me to consecrate myself totally to it. As you can see, I would prefer to bring my contribution to the rebirth of Haiti rather than to be added to the number of the martyrs of the second independence.

But to govern in Haiti often means to denounce a structure of corruption that will not crumble overnight. In Europe, it is not too difficult to criticize, but here it often means looking death in the face.

Has exercising power changed you?

I sometimes have the feeling that it caused me to grow in maturity. At the same time, my organism always rebels when it is confronted with frustration, anger, and the expectations of people who are assailed by suffering. All their cries penetrate me. How does one deal with the distress?

When I was inaugurated, it was because I had borne and shared in the sufferings of the people. The rebuff to my installation was something I had experienced throughout my priestly life, and even before my ordination. Beginning in 1976, several of my friends and I took an oath to refuse the comfort of a church of which we disapproved.

Our people are on the march. Whether their shepherd be a priest or a president, that person must ask himself or herself whether he or she is betraying them. I have no end in view other than to know how the people live, how they suffer, how they hope. I have to struggle unceasingly against distance, whether the distance of power or that of exile.

When the people make claims, you have usually taken their part, even as president . . .

This government is in a bad state. Let us say that it is a structure that has always set itself in opposition to the masses, has always crushed the little people. When you look at the different mechanisms, you always find that same mentality, that will to keep the same people at a distance. But the democratic arena should first of all allow each person to express herself or himself. My desire, as everyone knows, is to accept questioning, to understand the voices from below. I want the government to lose its repressive habits. It has to be made capable of listening, as I have done.

You are as popular as ever. What would your life be like if you were less so?

My attachment is to duty, not to popularity. I have no fear of any manipulations that might alter my relationship with the people. Even if I am not equal to satisfying all of their needs, I think that I am conducting a process of education in liberation. I have never said that the solution inevitably follows the claim, but I am open to the needs of all.

In the wake of the coup d'état, I am prepared to risk my popularity to prevent the spirit of revenge from thoroughly poisoning human and social relations.

As I said in August 1991, after the assembly of Croix-des-Bouquets: the government has to accept its responsibilities, and you have to check up on its representatives. Get into the machinery of the government, in order to do whatever is possible with it. The participation of people who are looking for solutions should dissipate the myth of a paternalist or inaccessible government. That is more necessary than ever after the dramatic military interlude.

During those eight months before the coup, did you sometimes feel yourself baffled by certain situations?

I by no means have solutions for everything, but I never felt myself boxed in. Is it my temperament, my formation in philosophy or psychology, the people around me, my own history? I think I have a certain predisposition to welcome events as they happen. I have never let myself be pushed around by history; I have always wanted to catch hold of it and guide it.

I am at the wheel of my own history. Flat tires or repairs are sometimes necessary, but it is I who am driving the car and not the other way around. People have to shape history and not be manipulated by it.

But surely a head of state has to make compromises?

Of course, but what do you mean by compromise? A head of state who steals makes compromises when he or she should be denouncing the thieves. A criminal head of state makes compromises with the mafia; a politician who sacrifices the national interest for personal profit or that of the oligarchy is in a poor position to negotiate. A frank and open life gives one a quite different kind of freedom! It does not prevent one from mediating or choosing, but even when the urgent and legitimate needs seem to be innumerable, it is easier that way.

In comparison with other heads of state in developing countries, you seem even today to be rather atypical.

In Haiti, we are watching the ascent of a rebellious people who are revolting against slavery. I am only the reflection, an echo of that movement. Our originality comes from the place occupied by the people: they are the principal actors. I simply try to exist in their dimension, to show that love and non-violence, through and beyond all the difficulties of life, are the only things that will enable us to go forward.

Too many of my colleagues hold their offices as a result of coups d'état or fixed elections. Here, the people have chosen their candidate and elected him without any dispute.

Have you already drawn some conclusions about your presidency? Do you feel any desire to continue, however that might occur, or to play a role in politics?

I hope to have the happiness of having prepared the ground and given comfort to democracy. I also desire that an honest and competent administration will allow me to depart with my conscience at peace.

After a term in office, if it had been exercised under normal conditions and carried out to the end, I could go on learning a great many things — in Haiti, in contact with the people. That relationship is, in itself, a kind of permanent university. Before being president, I was happy living where I was, in contact with the poorest of the poor, as one who learns and lives with the other.

Before I would change my mind, it would certainly have to happen that history would place me face to face with unexpected choices, such as the return of our people to their chains. Really, I can scarcely imagine myself at the head of a political party!

And an episcopal career?

I have no desire for it and I am not sure that anyone would suggest me for it! I see myself rather as a seeker, a friend of knowledge and of the philosophical quest, like Kant, a man who did so much to make philosophy critical. The know-how acquired in the practice of government sometimes expands in the direction of fundamental knowledge.

CHAPTER 16

Ten Commandments
of Democracy
in Haiti

As President of the Republic of Haiti, I enunciated these ten commandments in my speech to the General Assembly of the United Nations at New York, September 25, 1991:

... At the moment when the international community is absorbed in the shifting of the geopolitical axes of the planet, let us turn to our dear Haiti, that rebellious and faithful daughter,

> *Rebellious toward every imperialist dictate,*
> *Faithful to every democratic precept.*

Let us also speak primarily of ten glowing beacons christened "the ten commandments of democracy," arising out of our democratic praxis. Indeed, our message is limited to the democratic arena where they stand in a straight line, these "ten glowing beacons christened 'the ten commandments of democracy.' "

The first commandment of democracy: liberty or death.

As you know, Haiti was one of the first beacons of liberty

in the western hemisphere. In 1791 we presented to the world the first slave revolution, through which hundreds of thousands of blacks freed themselves from the yoke of oppression. The leaders of that victorious revolution helped to finance the liberating crusades of Simon Bolivar in South America. It was in Haiti that slavery was abolished for the first time: a giant step toward the liberation of humanity. The roots of the Declaration of Human Rights arose from the Haitian revolution. The Haiti of Boukmann, of Dessalines, of Toussaint-Louverture is and remains the first black republic in the world.

Haiti shone in the eyes of all as a star of liberty. Throughout our history, often glorious, sometimes troubled, we have always remembered with pride the unprecedented exploits of our ancestors. The cries of "Liberty or death, liberty or death," far from being stifled by a sterile past, have resounded steadily in the heart of a people who have become, forever, a free nation.

Throughout our long march toward 1991, in spite of our contribution to the free world, Haiti has never been able to open all the doors of the international community. The colonials of those days and their allies have been afraid of freedom: our leaders and the traditional oligarchy have feared it as well. From white colonials to black colonials, we have had to break the yoke of the black dictators and their international allies.

Happily, in 1986, to the astonishment of the whole world, the Haitian people overthrew a dictatorial regime that had lasted thirty years. That was the beginning of the end of a dictatorship whose marks are ineffaceable. The more those marks stare us in the face, the louder we cry out: "Liberty or death, liberty or death!"

The second commandment of democracy: democracy or death.

After having banished the oppressive and corrupt regime of the Duvaliers on February 7, 1986, at the end of that long and courageous struggle, the people of Charlemagne Péralte had only one choice: to install, once and for all, a democratic regime in Haiti. In that light, "liberty or death" is no different from "democracy or death." Hence we have conducted an unremitting struggle for the conquest of our rights against minority groups who have monopolized power since 1986. The struggle is unremitting and legitimate because that power has not worked to change the nature of a government that, for a long time, has created the objective conditions for maintaining the status quo and for sustaining the operation of the machinery of exploitation and oppression.

Finally, on December 16, 1990, thanks to the heroic courage of the Haitian people, thanks to their contribution, we for the first time carried out free, honest, and democratic elections! Honor to the Haitian masses! Glory to our ancestors, who put a stop to colonialism throughout the nineteenth century! Bravo to the international community! Bravo and applause to the United Nations!

Indeed, this was a great beginning in history. For once, through a brilliant tactical movement, a nation had carried out a revolution through the ballot box. The election of the president of the republic by more than 70 percent on the first ballot symbolized simultaneously

> *The victory of the people*
> *The power of the people*
> *The demands of the people.*

These free, honest and democratic elections are, in sum, the outcome of a strategy proper to us, that is to say, the historic rise of *Lavalas*. In union there is strength: is that not our slogan? With the fork of division, we said, no one can drink the soup of elections. In the same way, no one can drink the soup of democracy with the fork of division.

In a certain sense, the strategy of *Lavalas* corresponds to the thinking of the Pope who, in his encyclical *Centesimus Annus*, indicated that the events in Eastern Europe and in the Soviet Union are paving the way toward the reaffirmation of the "positive character of an authentic and integral theology of human liberation." In Haiti, this theological approach cannot be confined to a simple analysis of reality: it is meant to be, rather, a method and thought of action in the school of the poor, a priviledged site of the revelation of God, historical subject of that struggle for the integral liberation of humanity.

It is out of the actual experience of the poor that the pedagogy of democratic praxis arises, nourished and illuminated, of course, by liberation theology. The dialogue that must be established between the theology and politics of liberation necessarily passes by way of the experience of the poor.

When Jean-Paul Sartre, in criticizing Hegel, asserted that the latter forgot that the emptiness is empty of something, that is the point at which we, the theologians of liberation, can proclaim that the emptiness of the poor is receptive, is hungry, and it is not empty of what is essential.

Hungry for liberation—that emptiness suggests a legitimate expectation, the essence of which dwells in the spirit of the poor. It lives and gives life to democracy. It is for us who have been democratically elected to be faithful to their rights.

The third commandment of democracy: fidelity to human rights.

If human beings have duties, they certainly have rights: rights to respect and to be respected. It is, in the last analysis, to guarantee those rights that a just government is established.

The Universal Declaration of Human Rights is and remains sacred. It lays on us the heavy responsibility of faithfully obeying the constitutional mandate to "guarantee our inalienable and indefeasible rights to life, liberty and the pursuit of happiness," according to our Act of Independence of 1804 and the Universal Declaration of Human Rights of 1948.

We respect the Constitution on behalf of "a Haitian nation

that is socially just, economically free and politically independent."

We respect the Constitution for the sake of establishing an ideological pluralism and political succession, to strengthen national unity, to eliminate distinctions between city and country, to insure the harmonious separation and distribution of the powers of the executive, the judiciary and the parliament, that is, to install a governmental regime based on fundamental freedoms and respect for human rights, and to assure the cooperation and participation of the whole population in the great decisions involving the life of the nation through an effective decentralization.

The fourth commandment of democracy: the right to eat and to work.

It goes without saying that the right to eat is naturally included in the list of the rights belonging to every person. The reality of people who are starving because they are exploited is an immediate accusation against the oppressor as well as the authorities who are responsible for seeing that the inalienable and indefeasible rights of life are respected.

In Haiti, the victims have difficulty eating because they themselves are being eaten by the international axes of exploitation.

With respect to the arms race, "all countries taken together devote more than $500 billion dollars per year, i.e., one billion four hundred million dollars per day. With only fifteen days of this expenditure, it would be possible to eliminate hunger throughout the planet for several years."

The drama of the starving has nothing to do with a lack of food, but rather with a lack of social justice. Work, work, and more work: that is what they need to earn their bread by the sweat of their brows. Some people have shown that if, instead of a single B1 bomber, one were to build houses, for the same amount of money one could employ seventy thousand people.

How can we justify the fact that 71 percent of Haitian

farmers cultivate plots of less than 1.2 square hectares?

How can we justify the fact that, in our country, 3 percent of the richest landowners possess more than two-thirds of the arable land?

Certainly, we have to get past the traditional indifference of the dominant political and economic sectors in order to demand respect for the right to eat and to work. The hunger of one person is the hunger of humanity itself.

Work for everyone in and for a civilization based on work — in that way we can strike at the roots of hunger. The hunger of one person is the hunger of humanity itself.

In order to get beyond the limitations of language, let us explore a few trails of reality going back to February 7, 1991. In fact, since that date, the government of *Lavalas* has begun to bring order into our administration. The resources of the government have increased sharply. . . .

But an increase in food production has proved to be indispensable. To achieve that, we are undertaking the agrarian reform envisaged by the Constitution, Article 248, and placing at the disposal of the peasants the necessary framework within which they can produce.

The participation of the private sector is essential for the creation of highly labor-intensive industries. While in the past illicit practices have enabled certain sectors to despoil the country at the expense of the majority of the population, our *Lavalas* government, on the contrary, is on the alert to see that the rights of all are respected. These include the right to invest according to the constitutional norms, and the right to work for human and economic growth. To you, our dear friends and foreign investors, Haiti desires, now and in the future, to extend the warmest and most cordial welcome.

The fifth commandment of democracy: the right to demand what rightfully belongs to us.

"PA N SE PA N. PA N PA PA W " ("What belongs to us is ours. Ours is not yours").

The contribution of the Haitian people to the democratic

struggle that has been set in motion throughout the last five years all over the world is remarkable and exceptional.

At the intersection of the democratic streams of Eastern Europe, Asia, the Middle East, South Africa, Central and South America, there erupted among us, in Haiti, a democratic avalanche christened *lavalas*. No democratic nation can exist by itself, without weaving geopolitical, diplomatic, economic and international connections.

Today we are recording our right to demand what is rightfully ours in the context of that network of relationships where we have first acknowledged the fruits of a rich but impoverished past. Today we also acknowledge the fruits of a present that is exploited but the bearer of hope, and this thanks to the possibility of reconciling a colonized past with a democratic present.

Heraclitus of Ephesus rightly said: "People who are awake have only one world, but those who are asleep each have a world of their own."

As Haitian women and men who are awake, we have one world: the world of justice. Justice for everyone: for Haitians, women and men, too often the victims of social injustice at the international level! If we scan the horizons of this world of justice we wonder how long the impoverished will have to cry out with Democritus: "We seek the good and do not find it; we find evil without seeking it."

Convinced that *mens agitat molem* (the Spirit moves the mass), our politics remain alert and attentive to the masses whose voices demand, in respect and dignity, that which is owed to them. It arises out of the treatment inflicted on a great number of our Haitian sisters and brothers who are living in foreign lands.

The sixth commandment of democracy: legitimate defense of the diaspora, or tenth department.

Driven out until 1991 by the blind brutality of the repressive machine or by the structures of exploitation erected in an anti-democratic system, our Haitian sisters and brothers have not always had the good fortune to find a promised land. Illegal because the brutes have not had the forethought to give their victims certificates of torture properly signed; illegal because they have had to travel as boat people or without being provided with legal documents, they have nevertheless made great contributions to the economic prosperity of their patrons, preferring to do all the hardest work rather than to take charity.

What shall we say to our sisters and brothers who are imprisoned at Krome and elsewhere? In the name of democracy, is there no room for bending a little with regard to their files and transforming their pain into joy? With a view to encouraging the authorities concerned to take steps in the direction of that hoped-for joy, we, the government of Haiti, are continually battling against fraudulent practices and the obtaining of fake visas on Haitian soil. At the same time, we condemn the flagrant violation of the rights of Haitians living in the Dominican Republic.

While acknowledging the sovereignty of the Dominican Republic, we denounce and energetically condemn that violation of human rights.

Haiti and the Dominican Republic are two wings of one bird, two nations that share the beautiful island of Hispaniola. Echoing the voice of all the victims whose rights have been mocked, committed to respect human rights in spite of the social problems and financial difficulties caused by the forced repatriation of our people, we insist on respecting the two wings of the bird. This is attested by the welcome Haiti offers to all those who cross its border: women and men, Haitians and Dominicans.

In solidarity with all disadvantaged minorities, we call for reparations both for the native-born citizens of the Dominican Republic and those born in Haiti, and for the Haitian citizens who are victims of this repatriation.

Here, it is not a matter of weeping when one realizes what is happening in the Dominican Republic; it is a question of defending human rights, in the name of the Haitian people, and in the name of all the men who are men all over the world and of all the women who are women all over the world. As a result, we Haitians will work together with our Dominican sisters and brothers to live in harmony and in constant dialogue. That is why, together with the Dominican citizens who do not agree with this manner of trampling on human rights, we Haitian men and women, we, the people of Haiti, declare to the world that we demand reparation.

We will always continue to work with the Dominican people as brothers and sisters to live in peace, but never, never will a human being worthy of the name bow his or her head when human rights are trampled underfoot as is now the case for Haitians born either in the Dominican Republic or in Haiti, Haitians of Dominican origin or Dominicans of Haitian origin. It is regrettable that the question of color enters the picture, even when the people in question are Dominicans.

Arrested and expelled to Haitian territory, they ordinarily have neither roof, nor family, nor employment. Already, conservative estimates set the number of repatriates at more than fifty thousand. In the hope that the international bodies concerned will help us to ensure that the fundamental rights of the person are respected, now and hereafter, and that they will act in solemn fashion, we proclaim with pride and dignity that:

> *Never again*
> *Never again*
> *will our Haitian sisters and brothers*
> *be sold*
> *to convert their blood into bitter sugar.*

Let us always walk together with our Dominican brothers and sisters in dialogue, for the protection of the rights of all human beings, Dominicans and Haitians! To my Dominican sisters and brothers whom I love so much, I say: let us go forward together to build this peaceful world.

Seventh commandment of democracy: No to violence, yes to
Lavalas.

A political revolution without armed force in 1991: is it possible? Yes. Incredible, but true. The pedagogy of *Lavalas,* the tactical and strategic convergence of democratic forces, brandished the weapon of unity against that of violence. A stunning victory! An historic surprise!

Schooled by the poor, the pedagogy of active nonviolence and unity triumphed over institutionalized violence. After 1804, the date of our first independence, 1991 opened the era of our second independence.

Does there exist a democratic nation that is capable of remaining indifferent to that victory of nonviolence precisely in the place where the structures of economic violence still hold sway? Is it right to test the patience of the victims of economic violence? If there is no such thing as a politics unconnected with force, neither is there such a thing as an economy unconnected with interests.

The capital of nonviolence that the Haitians have already invested represents considerable economic interests, thanks to the restoration of peace. A simple social-psychological approach speaks volumes. In fact, the less the social self is under attack by the antiquated oligarchy, the more psychological, political and economic health it enjoys.

The pedagogy of nonviolence may support a collective raising of consciousness with regard to our country of nonviolence — a nonviolent country where, nevertheless, 85 percent of the population, crushed under the weight of economic violence, is still illiterate: illiterates who are not animals. Teaching these victims to read, today, is a challenge to the true friends of the Haitian people: I am not speaking of friends, but of true friends. You who are our true friends, do not be observers. Be actors, inasmuch as you are citizens of the world.

Together, let us participate in a campaign for literacy. Can we count on your cooperation? We hope so. All cooperation at this level testifies to a willingness to struggle against economic violence through active nonviolence.

Where the cannon of violence are roaring, that is where the sun of nonviolence is shining, *"lavalassement."*

The eighth commandment of democracy: fidelity to the human being, the highest form of wealth.

To speak of the human being as the highest form of wealth may imply that we are forgetting gold, oil, or greenbacks. Far from it. There is wealth, and then there is wealth. According to certain experts, if America's hydroelectric potential were fully exploited, it would be able to furnish more energy than all the oil that is consumed by the whole world.

All this wealth should be at the service of human beings, the pivot on which the whole politics of *lavalas* turns. We, too, are ready to prove our fidelity to humanity, embracing everything that promotes its full development. Hence the harmonious ties already fashioned with CARICOM are located within the framework of Caribbean solidarity for the purpose of better promoting human well-being.

We are also working at the intersection of our south-south relations, between our neighbors in South America and ourselves. South-south relations are not the only important ones for Haiti. In fact, we share a political heritage with the United States, whose independence reminds us of the Haitian pioneers who, precisely for the sake of that independence, were beaten and killed. Like France, with which we also share a political heritage together with the United States, the other countries of North America, Europe, the Middle East, Africa, and other parts of the globe are situated together with us within the network of interdependence that binds all the nations of the globe.

We offer patriotic greetings to the Haitian women and men living in Cuba, without forgetting Cuba and the Cuban people to whom we express our wishes for peace and growth in democracy.

We want to address these same wishes for peace and growth in democracy to the Middle East and South Africa.

United with all the blacks of Africa who are called to enjoy all the rights recognized by the Universal Declaration of Human Rights, we take advantage of this occasion to ask the international community, and especially the industrialized countries, not to lift too soon the global sanctions imposed against the government in Pretoria. Diametrically opposed to apartheid, the Republic of Haiti is striving to see that the black majority in South Africa may have full enjoyment of its rights in a multiracial, democratic society. Bravo Mandela! Honor to Mandela!

If the name of Mandela excites such applause, certainly another man deserves to be applauded as well: I am speaking of Martin Luther King.

The Haitian government has noted with satisfaction the cease-fire recently adopted between the parties to the conflict in the western Sahara, and reiterates its support for the process now at work. The suffering of one human being is the suffering of humanity. Our politics intends to offer, day by day, an eloquent witness to that fidelity: fidelity to humanity.

The ninth commandment of democracy: fidelity to our culture.

Lavalas interlaces the cultural bonds at the very heart of the political universe. Resistance to cultural alienation guarantees the psychological health of the democratic tissue. In fact, every kind of cultural suicide results in deviance in the social body and inevitably threatens the democratic cells.

To live, and to live fully, also means nourishing oneself at the sources of one's culture; it means plunging the roots of one's being into those sources.

Those cultural sources incorporate the whole life of a people. We are speaking of a density of nature that has to be studied and explored. By that nature we mean a fabric of multidimensional relationships. Defining the human being not as an end but as a bridge, Friedrich Nietzsche situated humanity, whether that was his intention or not, at the intersection of acculturation and inculturation. It is a question of the transmission of cultural seeds capable of vivifying or wounding a being in its very essence.

The seeds of pathological guilt transmitted by contact between the cultures that are called dominant and dominated can only injure any democratic encounter.

The politics of *lavalas* endeavors to validate our cultural identity. No truly deep change can be accomplished democratically without an articulation of the indigenous values that are closely linked with any genuine socio-cultural fabric.

That fidelity to the culture of humanity invites us to share the concerns of the Kurdish people, the Palestinian people, the Jewish people, the peoples of Iraq—all of them firmly attached to the roots of their own being.

In this perspective of respect and of peace, the Republic of Haiti rejoices greatly at the imminent admission of the two Koreas to the family of the United Nations.

Fidelity to our culture urges us to sharpen our critical sense in order to protect the health of our culture against certain plagues, such as the illicit traffic in narcotics. The Haitian government is resolved to recall that an effective struggle against the production of drugs is also conditional on the extension of stronger assistance to the Latin American countries.

As concerns the drug traffic itself, it is important to recall that it is generated and fed by the demands of the North. It is also necessary, at all costs, to eliminate the incentives to production coming from consumers in the industrialized countries. Concerted action involving governments North and South, aided by the United Nations, would permit us to conduct a more effective struggle against this plague of assorted drugs that is eating away at men and women.

The tenth commandment of democracy: everyone around the same table.

Yes, everyone around the democratic table
Not a minority on the table

Not a majority under the table
But everyone around the same table.

That, I think, is the historic meeting place as we approach 1992; on the eve of the celebration of five hundred years of evangelization for more than one country, but primarily and before all, of resistance on the part of us Haitians, women and men. For throughout those five hundred years we have resisted in order to follow and protect our freedom and our dignity. That is why, on the eve of the celebration of these five hundred years, which we call the five centuries of resistance — quantitative and qualitative — we can speak of this gathering around the table. It is truly and genuinely a challenge to be accepted on the threshold of the third millennium.

Sisters and brothers of Jamaica, Barbados, Trinidad, Cuba, the Dominican Republic, Guadeloupe, Martinique: our past struggle against colonialism has led us inevitably toward the establishment of deeper ties in the course of our long march toward the democratic table.

A new social contract at the Caribbean, Latin American and international level is clearly necessary for us to join together one day, all of us, around the democratic table.

We others in Haiti, since December 16, 1990, the date of our elections under the supervision of the United Nations, are on the march toward that meeting place.

To get there — and so that we may all get there — it is time that indebtedness cease to be the condition that governs the net transfer of the resources of our impoverished countries to the rich nations — I do not talk about "developed countries," but rather "countries that are called developed" — a transfer that has increased to the level of $115 billion. For the single year 1989, that transfer reached almost $60 billion — financial resources that the southern countries need absolutely for their own growth.

Mr. President,
I want to hope that the Fourth Decade of Development

will produce concrete results in the realm of the new international order that is to be inaugurated.

Here at the end of the twentieth century, the Republic of Haiti renounces absolutism, embraces participatory democracy, and intones the hymn of liberty, pride and dignity.

> *Liberty achieved!*
> *Pride restored!*
> *Dignity revived!*

Here at the end of the twentieth century, the Republic of Haiti has the honor to salute the United Nations.

> *Nations united*
> *For one world.*
> *Nations united*
> *By united peoples.*

As for the Haitian people, we again hail their heroic courage, crying "in the voice of Charlemagne Péralte," "in the voice of Dessalines," "in the voice of *Lavalas*":

> *It is better to perish with the people*
> *Than to succeed without the people*
> *But with the people,*
> *We know no defeat, so,*
> *Victory is ours!*

> *Pase pou nou reyisi san pèp la*
> *Pito nou echwe ak pèp le*
> *E ak pèp la, nou pap echwe.*

And again,

> *We believe in humanity.*
> *Wherever a human being is exploited,*
> *Call out to us.*

*At your call, we answer "yes," seventy-seven times
    "yes"*
*To exploitation, we answer "no," seventy-seven times
    "no."*
To defend human rights
Is the mission of the United Nations.

We believe in peace.
Where war is raging,
Call out to us.
*At your call, we answer "yes," seventy-seven times
    "yes"*
To war, we answer "no," seventy-seven times "no."
To guarantee the peace
Is the mission of the United Nations.

*We believe in the brotherhood, the sisterhood of peo-
    ples.*
Where whole peoples are excluded, disenfranchised,
Call out to us.
*At your call, we answer "yes," seventy-seven times
    "yes"*
*To exclusion, to disenfranchisement, we answer "no,"
    seventy-seven times "no."*
To be a place of dialogue
Is the mission of the United Nations.

We believe in the Haitian people.
Where they are struggling lavalas-*ly,*
We are there and we will always be there.
It is better to perish with the people
Than to succeed without the people.

While holding fast
To the echo of this credo
By way of a conclusion
Let us hold fast
To the echo of the credo of democracy.

Thus let it be
In the name of the People
And of their Children
And of their Holy Spirit
AMEN!

United, we are strong.
United in the Caribbean, we are a power
United in the world, we are a power
*   for Peace, for Justice, for Love and for Liberty.*

Do we have the right to speak here? If so, let us speak together, like the echoes resounding in Haiti:

YON SÈL NOU FÈB
ANSANM NOU FÒ
ANSANM ANSANM NOU SE LAVALAS

Alone we are weak
Together we are strong
All together we are lavalas.